Contents

How to Use This Book

You need only to memorize 100 French words in order to speak over 500 of the most useful phrases. To take full advantage of this concept please follow these simple steps:

- Memorize the vocabulary in the **100 Words section** in the beginning of the book. The words have been organized in groups to make it easier for you to memorize them. You'll notice that the verbs listed in the 100 Words section aren't fully conjugated. You'll need only the verb forms listed in this book to make 500+ phrases.

- You memorize only 100 words but your basic vocabulary actually consists of more since you are able to create compound words. The important ones are also listed in the **100 Words section**, others will be explained in tip boxes or footnotes. The abbreviation for singular is *sing.*, for plural *pl.*, for formal *form.* and informal *inform.* Masculine forms are indicated by ♂, feminine forms by ♀.

- The **100 Words section** as well as each individual chapter contain **Language Tip** boxes in red explaining important rules with examples.

- **Country and Culture Tips**, in green, inform you about important customs and traditions in France.

- The Chapters are organized by topics, e.g. Accommodations. Each chapter provides you with the basic and most useful expressions to function in a variety of situations. At times, phrases are supplemented by illustrations.

- The **Dictionary** in the back of the book gives you all the French words and expressions used in this program.

- The phonetic system used in this book makes it easy to pronounce the French words. Simply read the words as you would read them in English.

Pronunciation

Consonants

Letter	Approximate Pronunciation	Example
ch	like *sh* in *shut*	**chercher**
ç	like *s* in *sit*	**ça**
g	1) before **e, i, y,** like *s* in *pleasure*	**manger**
	2) before **a, o, u,** like *g* in *go*	**garçon**
gn	like *ni* in *onion*	**ligne**
h	always silent	**homme**
j	like *s* in *pleasure*	**jamais**
qu	like *k* in *kill*	**qui**
r	rolled in the back of the mouth, rather like gargling	**rouge**
w	usually like *v* in *voice*	**wagon**

Vowels

a, à, â	between the *a* in *hat* and the *a* in *father*	**mari**
é or **ez**	like *a* in *late*	**été**
è, ê, e	like *e* in *get*	**même**
e	sometimes like *er* in *other*	**je**
i	like *ee* in *meet*	**il**
o	generally like *o* in *hot* but sometimes like *oa* in *soar*	**donner** **rose**
ô	like *oa* in *soar*	**Rhône**
u	like *ew* in *dew*	**cru**

Letters **b, c, d, f, k, l, m, n, p, s, t, v, x** and **z** are pronounced as in English.

Sounds Spelled with Two or More Letters

ai, ay, aient, ais, ait, aî, ei	can be pronounced like *a* in *late* or like *e* in *get*	**j'ai** **vais** **chaîne** **peine**
(e)au	similar to *oa* in *soar*	**chaud**
eu, eû, œu	like *ur* in *fur*, but with lips rounded, not spread	**peu**
euil, euille	like *uh* in *huh*, but without pronouncing the *h* and with a *y* sound added	**feuille**
ail, aille	like *ie* in *tie*	**taille**
oi, oy	like *w* followed by the *a* in *hat*	**moi**
ou, oû	like *o* in *move* or *oo* in *hoot*	**nouveau**
ui	like *wee* in *between*	**traduire**

Nasal Sounds

French contains nasal vowels. A nasal vowel is pronounced simultaneously through the mouth and the nose, transcribed in the pronunciation with N.

am, an	something like *arn* in *tarnish*	**tante**
em, en	generally like the previous sound	**entrée**
ien	sounds like *yan* in *yank*	**bien**
im, in, aim, ain, eim, ein	approximately like *ang* in *rang*	**instant**
om, on	approximately like *ong* in *song*	**maison**
um, un	approximately like *ang* in *rang*	**brun**

Liaison and Stress

When a word ending in a consonant is followed by one beginning with a vowel, the words are often run together, and the consonant is pronounced as if it began the following word.

All syllables in French are pronounced with more or less the same degree of stress (loudness).

100 Words

1 **oui** wee
yes

2 **non** nohN
no

3 **le** ♂ luh
la ♀ lah
les lay
the; him/it
the; she
the *pl.*; they *pl.*

4 **un** ♂ aN
une ♀ ewn
des day
one; a
one; a
added in pl. forms

Language Tip

In French the definite article is either feminine, *la* (the), or masculine, *le* (the). The plural form for both genders is *les* as in *la chambre/les chambres* (the bedroom/bedrooms, *le lit/les lits* (the bed/beds).
The same holds true for the indefinite article: *un* (one, a) is masculine and *une* (one, a) is feminine. For plural forms, *des* is added: *des magasins* (shops), *des chambres* (rooms). There is no English equivalent for *des*.

---

5 **ce** ♂ suh
cette ♀ set
this; that
this

Language Tip

If preceded by a vowel (*a, e, i, o, u, y*), *je* is shortened to *j'*, as in *j'ai* (I have).

6	**je** zhuh	I
7	**me** muh	me
8	**moi** mwah	(to) me
9	**tu** tew	you *sing. inform.*
10	**te** tuh	you *sing. inform.*
11	**toi** twah	(to) you *sing. inform.*
12	**il** eel	he/it
13	**elle** el	she
14	**se** suh	himself/herself/itself/oneself
15	**nous** noo	we; us
16	**vous** voo	you/yourselves *pl./sing. form.*
17	**votre** voh-truh	your/yours *pl./sing. form.*
18	**on** ohN	someone; we; one

Language Tip

The French distinguish between the formal *vous* and the informal *tu*. *Tu* is used when talking to relatives, good friends and children. *Vous* is appropriate when talking to strangers, adults or in official situations.

Language Tip

In spoken French the personal pronoun *on* (one/someone) often replaces the word *nous* (we) as in *On mange* (We eat). Even if the meaning is clearly in the plural, the verb that follows *on* must always take the singular form.

19	**Bonjour.** bohN-zhoor	Good day/Good morning.
20	**Bonsoir.** bohN-swah	Good evening. Good night. Good-bye.
21	**Salut.** sah-lew	Hello./Hi.
22	**Au revoir.** oh-ruh-vwah	Good-bye.
23	**Pardon.** pah-dohN	Excuse me./I'm sorry.
24	**merci** mair-see	thanks; thank you
25	**comment** kohN-mohN	how
26	**quand** kahN	when
27	**où** oo	where; where to
28	**combien** kohN-bee-aN	how much/how many
29	**quel** kel **quelle** kel	which ♂ which ♀
30	**que** kuh	that; which; what; as
31	**ça** sah	this; that
32	**tout** too	everything; all

33	**quelque chose** kel-kuh shohz	something
34	**rien** ree-aN	nothing
35	**ne ... pas** nuh ... pah	not

Language Tip

The negative in French is formed by encircling the conjugated verb with *ne ... pas* (not) as in: *Je ne mange pas* (I don't eat). If the verb starts with a vowel or a silent *h*, *ne* becomes *n'*. In spoken language *ne* is often omitted: *J'ai pas mangé* (I've not eaten) instead of saying *Je n'ai pas mangé*.

Further forms of negations are *ne ... plus* (not anymore), *ne ... rien* (nothing), *ne ... plus rien* (nothing any more), *ne ... que* (only). These are used in such sentences as: *Je n'ai plus besoin de toi* (I don't need you any more). *Aujourd'hui, je ne fais rien* (Today I'll do nothing). *Ce soir, je ne bois plus rien* (I will not drink anything anymore tonight). *Je n'aime que cette boisson* (I like only this drink).

36	**y** ee	(over) there
37	**ici** ee-see	here
38	**aujourd'hui** oh-zhoor-dwee	today
39	**demain** duh-maN	tomorrow
40	**tard** tahr	late
41	**loin** lwaN	far
42	**deux** duh	two

43	**plus** plew	more
44	**beaucoup** boh-koo	much; very
45	**très** treh	very
46	**trop** troh	too/over ...
47	**déjà** day-zhah	already
48	**mais** meh	but (instead)
49	**et** eh	and
50	**aussi** oh-see	also
51	**dans** dahN	in; on
52	**à** ah	to; in; until
53	**de** duh	from; of

Language Tip

When used in combination with the article *le* (the), *à* and *de* always become *au* and *du*. If you want to say that you are going to bed you say: *Je vais au lit* (I'm going to bed); if you need the bed, you'd say: *J'ai besoin du lit* (I need the bed).

54	**pour** poor	for; in order to ...
55	**en** ehN	in; to; at; of that
56	**avec** ah-vek	with
57	**la journée** lah zhoor-nay	day
58	**le soir** luh swah	evening
59	**la nuit** lah nwee	night

60 **l'heure** ♀ luhr time; hour

Language Tip

Before nouns that start with a vowel (*a, e, i, o, u, y*) or a silent *h*, the articles *le* (the ♂) and *la* (the ♀) always become *l'*, as in *l'heure* (the hour).

---

61 **la chambre** lah shahN- (bed-)room
bruh

62 **le lit** luh lee bed

63 **le repas** luh ruh-pah meal

64 **la boisson** lah bwahs-sohN drink; beverage

65 **le temps** luh tahN weather; time

Language Tip

Like in English, the plural in French is generally formed by adding *-s* to the noun: *le magasin–les magasins* (the shop–the shops). This added *-s* remains silent, however, when spoken. If the singular form of the noun ends already with *-s*, the singular and plural are identical: *un repas–deux repas* (one meal–two meals).

---

66 **la taille** lah tah-yuh size

67 **le cadeau** luh kah-doh present; gift

68	**les États-Unis*** lay-zay-tah-zewn-ee	United States
69	**le magasin** luh mah-gah-zaN	shop; store
70	**la ville** lah veel	city; town

Language Tip

The comparative and superlative of adjectives are formed with *plus* and *le plus*: *cher* (expensive), *plus cher* (more expensive), *le plus cher* (most expensive). When comparing something similar or equal, use the word *aussi*, as in *Pierre est aussi grand que Paul* (Pierre is as tall as Paul).

71	**bon** ♂ bohN	good
	bonne ♀ bun	good
72	**beau** ♂ boh	nice; handsome
	belle ♀ bel	nice; pretty
73	**grand** grahN	big; large
74	**petit** puh-tee	small
75	**content** kohN-tahN	content; happy
76	**cher** ♂ shair	expensive
	chère ♀ shair	expensive

---

* **la Grande-Bretagne** lah grahNd-bruh-tahn-yuh Great Britain
le Canada luh kah-nah-dah Canada

Language Tip

Adjectives agree in gender and number with the noun to which they refer: e.g. *un grand lit* (a large bed), *une grande chambre* (a big bedroom), *des grands magasins* (large shops). Most adjectives will have an *-e* added for the feminine form and an *-s* for the plural form. See the above adjective examples for some irregular forms that do not follow this rule, for example, *beau*.

77	**bien** bee-aN	good; nice
78	**mieux** myuh	better
79	**mal** mahl	bad
	Ça fait mal. sah feh mahl	It hurts.
	J'ai mal. zhay mahl	I'm in pain.
		It hurts me.
	Vous avez mal.	You are in pain. *pl./sing. form.*
	voo-zah-vay mahl	You are hurting. *pl./sing. form.*

Language Tip

The words *bien, mieux* and *mal* are adverbs. They describe how an action is performed: *Tu le fais bien* (You are doing this well). Their form never changes.

80 **être** eh-truh — to be
    je suis zhuh swee — I am
    tu es tew eh — you are *sing. inform.*
    il/elle est eel/el eh — he/she/it is
    vous êtes voo-set — you are *pl./sing. inform.*
    ils sont eel sohN — they are
    il/elle était eel/el ay-tay — he/she/it was

81 **avoir** ah-vwahr — to have
    j'ai zhay — I have
    tu as tew ah — you have *sing. inform.*
    nous avons — we have
    noosah-vohN
    vous avez voosah-veh — you have *pl./sing. form.*

82 **avoir besoin de** — to need
    ah-vwahr buh-zwaN duh
    nous avons besoin de — we need
    noosah-vohN buh-zwaN
    duh
    vous avez besoin de — you need *pl./sing. form.*
    voosah-veh buh-zwaN
    duh

83 **aider** ay-day — to help
    j'aide zhayd — I help

84 **arriver** ah-ree-veh — to arrive
    il/elle arrive eel/el ah-reev — he/she/it arrives
    vous arrivez — you arrive *pl./sing. form.*
    voo sah-ree-veh
    arrivé ah-ree-veh — arrived, happened

85 **passer** pah-say — to pass/walk by;
to spend (time)

  il/elle passe eel/el pahss — he/she passes by
  tu passes tew pahss — you pass by *sing. inform.*
  nous passons — we pass by
  noo pah-sohN
  vous passez voo pah-say — you pass by *pl./sing. form.*
  passé pah-say — passed; happened; spent time

Language Tip

The perfect tense is formed with the conjugated verbs *avoir* (to have) or *être* (to be) and the participle of the verb such as *arrivé* (arrived) or *passé* (spent time).

With verbs that form their perfect tense with *être*, the participle acts like an adjective where the feminine form has the ending *-e* and the plural the ending *-s* (*-es* with feminine plurals).

---

86 **aimer** em-ay — to want; to like
  j'aimerais zhem-eh-ray — I/you want
  nous aimerions — we want
  noosem-ehr-yohN
  vous aimeriez — you want *pl./sing. form.*
  voo sem-ehr-yay

87 **cassé** kah-say — broken; damaged
burst; torn

88 **manger** mahN-zhay — to eat
  je mange zhuh mahNzh — I eat
  tu manges tew mahNzh — you eat *sing. inform.*
  vous mangez — you eat *pl./sing. form.*
  voo mahN-zhay

89 **acheter** ahsh-tay — to buy

90 **appeler** ahp-lay — to call
    il/elle appelle — he/she calls (on the phone)
    eel/el ah-pel
    appelé aph-lay — called
    je m'appelle — I am called (my name is)
    zhuh mah-pel
    tu t'appelles — you are called *sing. inform.*
    tew tah-pel
    nous nous appelons — we are called
    noo noosahp-lohN
    vous vous appelez — you are called *pl./sing. form.*
    voo voosah-play

Language Tip

Regular verbs ending with *-er* like *aimer* (to love) form their present tense by replacing the ending *-er* with *-e, -es, -e, -ons, -ez, -ent*: *j'aime* (I love), *tu aimes* (you love), *il/elle aime* (he/she loves), *nous aimons* (we love), *vous aimez* (you love), *ils/elles aiment* (they love).

---

91 **faire** fair — to do; to make; to cost
    je fais zhuh feh — I make
    tu fait tew feh — you make *sing. inform.*
    nous faisons — we make
    noo fuh-zohN
    vous faites voo fet — you make *pl./sing. form.*
    ils/elles font eel/el fohN — they make
    fait feh — made

92 **pouvoir** poo-vwah — can; to be able to
   je peux zhuh puh — I can
   il/elle peut puh — he/she/it can
   nous pouvons — we can
   noo poo-vohN
   vous pouvez — you can *pl./sing. form.*
   voo poo-veh
   je pouvais — I could/was able to
   zhuh poo-vay

93 **prendre** prahN-druh — to take
   je/tu prends — I/you take *sing. inform.*
   zhuh/tew prahN
   nous prenons — we take
   noo pruh-nohN
   vous prenez — you take *pl./sing. form.*
   voo pruh-nay
   pris pree — taken

94 **ouvre** oov-ruh — open(s)
   ouvert oo-vair — open

95 **boire** bwahr — to drink
   je/tu bois — I/you drink *sing. inform.*
   zhuh/tew bwah
   vous buvez — you drink *pl./sing. form.*
   voo bew-veh
   bu bew — drunk

96 **perdre** pair-druh — to lose
   perdu pair-dew — lost; misplaced

97 **plaît** pleh — please; like
   s'il te plaît — please *sing. inform.*
   seel-tuh-pleh
   s'il vous plaît — please *pl./sing. form.*
   seel-voo-pleh

98 **voir** vwahr to see
  je/tu vois I/you see *sing. inform.*
  zhuh/tew vvah
  il/elle voit eel/el wvah he/she sees
  nous voyons we see
  noo vwah-yohN
  vous voyez you see *pl./sing. form.*
  voo vwah-yeh
  vu vew seen

99 **dire** deer to say
  je/tu dis zhuh/tew dee I/you say *sing. inform.*
  il/elle dit eel/el dee he/she/it says
  vous dites voo deet you say *pl./sing. form.*

100 **aller** ah-lay to go; to drive
  je vais zhuh veh I go
  tu vas tew vah you go *sing. inform.*
  il/elle va eel/el vah he/she/it goes
  nous allons we go
  noo zah-lohN
  vous allez voo sah-lay you go *pl./sing. form.*
  allé ah-lay gone

Language Tip

Like in the English "going to", the verb *aller* can be used to form the future tense by combining the present tense of *aller* and the infinitive of the main verb. This type of future is used to express an intention or an action that will take place in the immediate future: *Je vais manger* means "I am about/I'm going to eat".

Meeting people

Greetings

This greeting can be used at any time of the day:

Salut. sah-lew   Hello.

Use these at a particular time of day:

Bonjour. bohN-zhoor   Good day.
                                     Good morning.

Bonsoir. bohN-swah   Good evening.
                                     Goodnight.

Country and Culture Tip

If you want to address someone whose last name you
know, say *Monsieur ...* (mesyewr) to a man, *Madame ...*
(mah-dahm) to a married woman and *Mademoiselle ...*
(mahd-mwah-zel, which also means woman) to a younger
woman.

If you do not know the name of the person, but want to
address that person politely you could simply say *Bonjour
Monsieur! Bonjour Madame!* or *Bonjour Mademoiselle!*

Saying Good-bye

To say good-bye in a formal setting say:

Au revoir. oh ruh-vwah   Good-bye.

Bonsoir. bohn-swah   Good-bye (in the evening).
                                     Good night.

Country and Culture Tip

Bonjour is the greeting used in France throughout the morning, and can mean both "Good morning" and "Good day". *Bonsoir*, Good evening, can be used right through to the late hours of the night and serves as both a greeting and a farewell because *Bonsoir* also means "Good night". *Bonne nuit* (the literal "Good night") is only used when sending children to bed.

Salut can be used at any time of the day both as a greeting and a farewell. Bear in mind, though, that it is only used when you are on familiar terms with someone and address each other with the informal *tu* instead of the formal *vous*.

For a more informal greeting, try:

Salut. sah-lew	Bye.
A plus tard! ah plew tahr	See you later!
A plus! ah plewss	See you later!
A tout à l'heure!* ah too-tah luhr	See you soon! See you later!

---

* Idiomatic expression:
A tout à l'heure! ah too-tah luhr   See you soon!/See you later!

Country and Culture Tip

Generally the French use the formal address, *vous,* even if they add the personal surname afterwards.

The custom of shaking hands is limited to formal situations. Friends and relatives greet each other with a gentle kiss on both cheeks. This is done liberally both as a greeting and a farewell. The number of kisses exchanged varies from two to four, depending on the region and the closeness between the two individuals.

To be more precise about seeing each other again, you could say:

A ce soir! ah suh swah	Until this evening!
Au revoir, à demain! oh-ruh-vwah ah duh-maN	Good-bye! Until tomorrow!
On se voit demain! ohN suh vwah duh-maN	See you tomorrow!
A demain! ah duh-maN	Until tomorrow!
A demain soir! ah duh-maN swah	Until tomorrow evening!
A une heure! ah ewn uhr	Until one o'clock!
A demain, une heure! ah duh-maN ewn uhr	Until tomorrow at one!
A deux heures! ah duh zuhr	Until two!
A demain, deux heures! ah duh-maN duh-zuhr	Until tomorrow at two!

A ... [number] heures! ah ... uhr   Until ... o'clock!

A demain, ... [number] heures!   Until tomorrow at ... !
ah duh-maN ... uhr

Language Tip

The French prefer using the 24-hour time scale to avoid any misunderstandings. See page 111 for numbers.

A ... [day of week]! ah   Until ...!

See page 112 for days of the week.

If you want to meet at a specific location, you can say:

On se voit au ... ohN suh vwah oh   We'll see each other
at the ...

restaurant   **bar**   **café**   **théâtre**
res-toh-rahN   bahr   kah-feh   tay-ah-truh

Country and Culture Tip

A *café* serves a wide variety of drinks, but as far as food, it offers only snacks such as chips, peanuts, toast or sandwiches.

A *café-bar-tabac* has a very limited number of tables for seating as most visitors will stand at the bar counter. These bars also sell cigarettes.

A *salon de thé* offers coffee, teas and cakes, pastries and ice-cream.

A *restaurant* is the true place for eating out. When you go to a *restaurant* make sure to wait to be seated.

Here are a few farewells:

Bonne journée! bun zhoor-nay

Have a nice day!

A toi aussi, merci!
ah twah oh-see mair-see

Thanks, you too!
sing. inform.

A vous aussi, merci!
ah voo oh-see mair-see

Thank you, the same to you! *pl./sing. form.*

Language Tip

Vous (you) is used both for the second person plural as well as for the formal and polite version of you, singular and plural. The same applies for *votre* (your/their).

Introductions

To introduce yourself or someone else, say:

Je m'appelle ... zhuh mah-pel   My name is (I'm called) ...

Je suis ... zhuh swee   I am ...

Nous nous appelons ...   Our names are ...
noo noo zah-plohN

C'est ... [name of the person   This is ...
you want to introduce]. seh

Ce sont ... [names of the   These are ...
people you want to introcude].
suh sohN

If you want to find out the name of the person you are talking to:

Comment t'appelles-tu?   What's your name?
kohN-mohN tah-pel tew   *sing. inform.*

Comment vous appelez-vous?   What is your name/are
kohN-mohN vou zah-play voo   your names? *sing. form./pl.*

Moi, je m'appelle ... Et toi?   My name is ... And yours?
mwah zhuh mah-pel ... eh twah   *sing. inform.*

Moi, je m'appelle ... Et vous? My name is ... And yours?
mwah zhuh mah-pel ... eh voo   *sing. form./pl.*

Language Tip

In the previous sentences, *moi* was used as emphasis and to stress the subject of the sentences: *Moi, je m'appelle Pierre* (I am called Pierre).

Serving the same function, *moi* (I) and *toi* (you) can also be inserted at the end of the sentences *c'est—C'est toi, Pierre?* (Is that you, Pierre?)—or after prepositions such as *avec* (with) or *pour* (for) as in *avec toi* (with you), *pour toi* (for you).

If you forgot someone's name or did not understand it at first, just ask:

Pardon, mais comment t'appelles-tu déjà?
pah-dohN meh kohN-mohN tah-pehl tew day-zhah

Excuse me, but what is your name again? *sing. inform.*

Pardon, mais comment vous appelez-vous déjà?
pah-dohN meh kohN-mohN voo zah-play voo day-zhah

Excuse me, but what is your name/are your names again? *sing. form./pl.*

Comment est-ce que tu t'appelles déjà? kohN-mohN ess-kuh tew tah-pel day-zhah

What is your name again? *sing. inform.*

Comment est-ce que vous vous appelez déjà? kohN-mohN ess-kuh voo voo zah-play day-zhah

What is your name/ were your names again? *sing. form./pl.*

Peux-tu me dire comment tu t'appelles? puh tew muh deer kohN-mohN tew tah-pehl

Can you tell me your name? *sing. inform.*

Pouvez-vous me dire comment vous vous appelez?
poo-veh-voo muh deer
kohN-mohN voo voo zah-play

Can you tell me
your name/names?
sing. form./pl.

Language Tip

There are three ways to ask a question in French:
- By raising the intonation of your voice slightly at the end of the sentence: *Tu dis comment pour ça?*
- By putting the interrogative clause *est-ce que* in front of the statement, as in *Comment est-ce que tu dis pour ça?*
- By reversing the verb and the subject and inserting a hyphen between the two as in *Comment dis-tu pour ça?*
All three simply mean: "What is this called?"

Be aware that the French put a lot of emphasis on the correct pronunciation of names:

Tu le dis très bien.
tew luh dee treh bee-aN

You say it very nicely!
sing. inform.

Vous le dites bien!
voo luh deet bee-aN

You say it very well!
sing. form./pl.

Ce n'est pas mal.
suh neh pah mahl

That's not bad.

C'est très bien! seh treh bee-aN

That's very good!

Language Tip

The definite articles *le, la, les* or *l'* (before a vowel or silent *h*) can be used to replace a direct object. The article used must be the same in gender (♂, ♀) and number (sing./pl.) as the noun it is replacing: *Je vois le magasin – Je le vois* (I see the store – I see it).

Saying Thanks

Here are some general ways to say thanks:

Merci. mair-see	Thank you.
Merci pour tout. mair-see poor too	Thanks for everything.
Merci beaucoup. mair-see boh-koo	Thank you very much.
Merci beaucoup pour tout. mair-see boh-koo poor too	Many thanks for everything.
Un grand merci pour tout! aN grahN mair-see poor too	A big thank you for everything!
J'aimerais te dire un grand merci. zhem-reh tuh deer aN grahN mair-see	I want to thank you very much. *sing. inform.*
J'aimerais vous dire un grand merci pour tout. zhem-reh voo deer aN grahN mair-see poor too	I want to thank you very much for all that. *sing. form./pl.*
Comment est-ce que je peux te dire merci? kohN-mohN ess-kuh zhuh puh tuh deer mair-see	How can I ever thank you for that? *sing. inform.*

Comment est-ce que je peux vous dire merci? kohN-mohN ess-kuh zhuh puh voo deer mair-see

How can I ever thank you for that?
sing. form./pl.

The appropriate reply to the phrases above would be:

De rien! duh ree-aN

Don't mention it!

Oui, merci! wee mair-see

Yes, thank you!

Country and Culture Tip

In French *De rien* (Don't mention it!/It's nothing) is said only in reply to someone else's gratitude. If you want to confirm your acceptance of an offer with "Yes, please" say *Oui, merci*.

You may not always remember all of these intricacies, but do make sure to insert the obligatory *s'il vous plaît* or *s'il te plaît* with every request and question.

To thank people in other situations, you can say:

Merci de faire tout ça pour moi. mair-see duh fair too sah poor mwah

Thank you for doing all that for me.

Merci d'avoir fait ça pour moi. mair-see dah-vwah feh sah poor mwah

Thank you for all that you have done for me.

Language Tip

The perfect tense is formed with the conjugated auxiliary verb *avoir* (to have) or *être* (to be) and the main verb, as in *avoir fait* (to have done), *être allé* (to have gone).

Merci d'être avec moi.
mair-see det-ruh ah-vek mwah

Thank you for being with me.

Merci beaucoup de m'aider.
mair-see boh-koo duh may-day

Thank you very much for helping me.

Merci d'avoir pris le temps.
mair-see dah-vwah pree luh tahN

Thank you for taking the time.

Merci d'avoir passé beaucoup de temps avec moi.
mair-see dah-vwah pah-say boh-koo duh tahN ah-vek mwah

Thank you for spending so much time with me.

Merci de m'appeler.
mair-see duh mah-play

Thank you for your call.

Merci de passer me voir.
mair-see duh pah-say muh vwahr

Thank you for your visit.

Merci pour le bon temps passé avec vous! mair-see poor luh bohN tahN pah-say ah-vek voo

Thank you for the nice time I spent with you! *sing. form./pl.*

Merci pour cette bonne journée.
mair-see poor set bun zhoor-nay

Thank you for this beautiful day.

Language Tip

Use the word *merci* when you want to thank someone.
Merci de … is used before a verb: *Merci de m'appeler.*
(Thank you for calling.)
Merci pour … or occasionally *merci de …* is used in front of a noun: *Merci pour le bon repas.* (Thank you for the good meal.)

If you want to thank someone, but also want to express that they have gone overboard, try one of these phrases:

Merci beaucoup pour tout—mais c'est trop! mair-see boh-koo poor too meh seh troh
Many thanks for everything—but this is too much!

Merci pour tout—mais c'est beaucoup trop! mair-see poor too meh seh boh-koo troh
Many thanks for everything—but this is way too much!

Merci, mais tu en fais trop*! mair-see meh tew ahN feh troh
Many thanks, but you really did too much! *sing. inform.*

Merci, mais vous en faites trop*! mair-see meh voo zahN fet troh
Many thanks, but you really did too much! *sing. form./pl.*

---

* Idiomatic expressions:
   Tu en fais trop. tew ahN feh troh   You did too much. *sing. inform.*
   Vous en faites trop. voo zahN fet troh   You did too much. *sing. form./pl.*

You can also say thanks for specific things:

Merci pour ce beau cadeau.
mair-see poor suh boh cah-doh

Thanks for the nice present.

Merci beaucoup pour ce très beau cadeau. mair-see boh-koo poor seh treh boh cah-doh

Many thanks for this very nice present.

Merci pour ce bon repas.
mair-see poor suh bohN ruh-pah

Thank you for the good meal.

Merci pour ce bon ...
mair-see poor suh bohN

Thank you for the good ...

café
kah-feh

fromage
froh-mahzh

vin
vaN

spectacle
spek-tah-kluh

Communication Difficulties

If you find it difficult to understand what is being said simply ask:

Comment? kohN-mohN

Excuse me?

Que dis-tu? kuh dee tew

What did you say?
sing. inform.

Que dites-vous? kuh deet voo

What did you say?
sing. form./pl.

Qu'as-tu dit, s'il te plaît?
kah tew dee seel tuh pleh

What did you say, please?
sing. inform.

Qu'avez-vous dit, s'il vous plaît?
kah-veh voo dee seel voo pleh

What did you say, please? *sing. form./pl.*

Language Tip

In the previous examples the word *que* was used as interrogative term (what): *Que vois-tu?* (What do you see?) Keep in mind, though, that in front of a vowel *que* becomes *qu'*, as in *Qu'as-tu dis?* (What did you say?)

If you wish to consult this guide to look up an expression and want someone to wait for a moment, say:

J'aimerais dire quelque chose.
zhem-ray deer kel-kuh shohz

I want to say something.

J'ai besoin de temps pour dire quelque chose.
zhay buh-zwaN duh tahN poor deer kel-kuh shohz

I need a moment to say it.

The person may reply:

Prends le temps! prahn luh tahN

Take your time!

Prenez votre temps!
pruh-nay voh-truh tahN

Take your time!
sing. form./pl.

Moi aussi, j'ai le temps.
mwah oh-see zhay luh tahN

I have time, too.

Mais prends le temps!
meh prahN luh tahN

Please take your time!
sing. inform.

Language Tip

The previous sentences were given in the imperative. In French the imperative for regular verbs ending in *-er* is formed like the following forms of the present tense of the verb *aider*: *Aide!* (Help! *sing. inform.*) *Aidez!* (Help! *sing. form./pl.*) Other verbs such as *prendre* (to take) have special forms: *Prends!* (Take it! *sing. inform.*) *Prenez!* (Take it! *sing. form./pl.*)

You can expand your vocabulary by learning new words. If you want to know the name of something, point at it and ask:

Qu'est-ce que c'est?
kess-kuh seh

What's that?

C'est un ...? ♂
set aN

Is that a ...?

C'est une ...? ♀
set ewn

Is that a ...?

Comment dis-tu pour ça, s'il te plaît?
kohN-mohN dee-tew poor sah seel tuh pleh

What is this called, please? *sing. inform.*

Comment dites-vous pour ça, s'il vous plaît? kohN-mohN deet-voo poor sah seel voo pleh

What is this called, please? *sing. form./pl.*

Aide-moi à dire ça.
ed-mwah ah deer sah

Help me say this. *sing. inform.*

Aidez-moi à le dire!
ed-ay mwah ah luh deer

Help me to say it! *sing. form./pl.*

If you are met with an air of surprise or bewilderment, you may have said something incorrectly. Ask what you did wrong:

Ce n'est pas un ...♂
[repeat the word]?
suh neh pah-zaN

Isn't that a ...?

Ce n'est pas une ...♀
[repeat the word]?
suh neh pah-zewn

Isn't that a ...?

Ce n'est pas du tout ça, non?
suh neh pah dew too sah nohN

This was completely
wrong, wasn't it?

Language Tip

In combination with a negative clause the term *tout* (all, everything) stresses negation; *ne ... pas du tout,* therefore, means "not at all" as in *Je ne bois pas du tout.* (I don't drink at all.)

Pardon, mais je n'arrive pas
bien à le dire.
pah-dohN meh zhuh nah-reev
pah bee-aN ah luh deer

I'm sorry, but I can't
manage to say this
correctly.

Oui, je vois. wee zhuh vwah

Yes, I see.

Non, je ne vois pas.
nohN zhuh nuh vwah pah

No, I don't see.

Small Talk

Health

It is common to ask about people's well-being, even if you do not expect a lengthy answer.

Comment vas-tu?
kohN-mohN vah-tew

How are you? *sing. inform.*

Comment allez-vous?
kohN-mohN tah-lay voo

How are you?
sing. form./pl.

In a more informal setting you could also ask:

Ça va? sah-vah

What's up?

Comment ça va?
kohN-mohN sah vah

How's it going?

Comment vas-tu aujourd'hui?
kohN-mohN vah tew
oh-zhoor-dwee

How is it going today?
sing. inform.

**Comment allez-vous
aujourd'hui?** kohN-mohN
tah-lay voo oh-zhoor-dwee

How are you doing today?
sing. form./pl.

Country and Culture Tip

Many conversations in French start with *Comment allez-vous?* or, informally, *Comment vas-tu?* Good friends or relatives simply greet each other with *Ça va?*
You can reply with *Ça va* (Fine), and you can also ask *Et vous?* or *Et toi?* A typical conversation might go like this:
– *Ça va?*
– *Oui, ça va. Et toi, ça va?*
– *Très bien, merci.*

If someone has been going through a hard time lately, you could ask:

Ça va mieux?
sah vah myuh

Are you feeling better?

Tu vas mieux aujourd'hui?
tew vah myuh oh-zhoor-dwee

Are you feeling any better today? *sing. inform.*

Vous allez mieux aujourd'hui?
voo zah-lay myuh oh-zhoor-dwee

Are you feeling any better today? *sing. form./pl.*

Demain, ça va aller mieux.
duh-maN sah vah ah-lay myuh

You'll feel better tomorrow.

Tu vas déjà mieux?
tew vah day-zhah myuh

Are you better already? *sing. inform.*

Vous allez déjà mieux?
voo zah-lay day-zhah myuh

Are you better already? *sing. form./pl.*

Aujourd'hui, c'est déjà mieux.
oh-zhoor-dwee seh day-zhah myuh

Things are already better today.

Aujourd'hui, c'est déjà beaucoup mieux. oh-zhoor-dwee seh day-zhah boh koo myuh

Things are already much better today.

Language Tip

You are probably asking yourself why some sentences contain two forms of the verb *aller* (to go) as in *Demain, ça va aller mieux.* (You will feel better tomorrow.) This is the immediate future tense that is formed with *aller*, used as an auxiliary verb. *Aller* is conjugated in the present tense and combined with the infinitive form of the main verb, in this case, again, *aller*. The English equivalent for this form is "I am going to go".

Inquiries about someone's well-being are usually answered positively:

Très bien, merci.
treh bee-aN mair-see

Very well, thank you.

Je vais bien, merci.
zhuh veh bee-aN mair-see

I am doing well,
thank you.

Ça va, merci. sah vah mair-see

Fine, thanks.

Ça va. sah vah

Fine.

Oui. Et toi? wee eh twah

Fine. And you? *sing. inform.*

Oui, merci. Et vous?
wee mair-see eh voo

Fine, thanks. And you?
sing. form./pl.

Ça ne peut pas aller mieux!
sah nuh puh pah ah-lay myuh

Things couldn't be better!

Je vais de mieux en mieux*.
zhuh veh duh myuh zahN myuh

Things are getting better
and better.

Ça ne va pas trop mal.
sah nuh vah pah troh mahl

Not too bad.

Tout va bien. too vah bee-aN

Everything is OK.

There are times when the answer might be less positive:

Pas très bien. pah treh bee-aN

Not very well.

Pas bien du tout.
pah bee-aN dew too

Not good at all.

Ça ne va pas. sah nuh vah pah

I'm in bad shape.

---

* Idiomatic expression:
  de mieux en mieux duh myuh zahN myuh   better and better

Ça ne va pas du tout. sah nuh vah pah dew too	I'm miserable.
Non, ça ne va pas bien. nohN sah nuh vah pah bee-aN	No, I'm not feeling well.
Tout va mal. too vah mahl	Everything is going wrong.
Non, ça ne va pas mieux. nohN sah nuh vah pah myuh	No, I'm not feeling better.
Ça peut aller. sah puh ah-lay	Just OK.
Je ne vais pas bien. zhuh nuh veh pah bee-aN	I'm not feeling well.

Background

One of the first questions you'll ask is where someone comes from:

D'où es-tu? doo eh tew	Where are you from? *sing. inform.*
D'où êtes-vous? doo et voo	Where are you from? *sing. form./pl.*

Language Tip

If you want to ask someone where he/she is from, say: *D'où es-tu?* (Where are you from?) *D'où* is formed by combining *de* (from) and *où* (where). Because the second word starts with a vowel (o), *de* is shortened to *d'*.

Je suis des États-Unis*.
zhuh swee day-zay-tah-zew-nee

I'm from the
United States.

Et où en États-Unis?
eh oo ahN zay-tah-zew-nee

And from where in the
United States?

Je suis de … [name of city].
zhuh swee duh

I'm from …

C'est loin de … [city]?
seh lwaN duh

Is that far from …?

**Non, ce n'est pas très
loin de … [city].**
nohN suh neh pah treh lwaN
duh

No, that's not very
far from …

Language Tip

In French, country names are generally preceded by *en* and
city names by *à*. These prepositions are used no matter
whether one is already in the place or location or is about to
travel there:
Je suis en Angleterre. – Je vais en Angleterre
(I am in England. – I'm going to England.)
Il est à New York. – Il va à New York.
(He is in New York. – He is going to New York.)

---

* **de Grande-Bretagne** duh grahNd bruh-tahn-yuh   from Great Britain
du Canada dew kah-nah-dah   from Canada

SMALL TALK

Maybe the person you're talking to has already visited your country:

J'y suis déjà allé! ♂
zhee swee day-zhah ah-lay

I've been there already!

J'y suis déjà allée! ♀
zhee swee day-zhah ah-lay

I've been there already!

Je suis déjà allé en …
[country] zhuh swee
day-zhah ah-lay ahN

I've already been
to …

Je suis déjà allé à …
[city] zhuh swee
day-zhah ah-lay ah

I've already been
to …

J'aime beaucoup cette ville.
zhem boh-koo set veel

I like that city very much.

J'aimerais beaucoup y aller!
zhem-reh boh-koo pee ah-lay

I would like to go there
one day!

J'aime bien les États-Unis*.
zhem bee-aN lay zay-tah-
zew-nee

I like the United States
very much.

**Nous aimons beaucoup
les États-Unis*!**
noo zem-ohN boh-koo
lay-zay-tah-zew-nee

We like the United States
very much!

---

* **la Grande-Bretagne** lah grahNd bruh-tahn-yuh   Great Britain
le Canada luh kah-nah-dah   Canada

42

Language Tip

The previous phrases with *je suis allé* (I've been) are in the perfect tense. Just like in English, the perfect tense consists of two parts: the conjugated auxiliary verb *avoir* (to have) or *être* (to be) and the main verb (here: *allé* – gone).

With verbs that form their perfect tense with *être* as the auxiliary verb, the main verb is treated like an adjective, meaning it must agree with the subject of the sentence. In the case of *je suis allé* a man is speaking, while *je suis allée* means that the sentence is said by a woman.

Nous sommes allés means that more than one person is speaking while in *nous sommes allées* more than one woman (in a group of only women) is speaking. As with all other adjectives the female form has an *-e* and the plural has *-s* added at the end of the word.

Dans cette ville, j'aime les magasins! daN set veel zhem lay mahghah-saN	I love this city for its shops!
Dans cette ville, j'aime les …! daN set veel zhem lay	I love this city for its …!

hôtels
oh-tel

restaurants
res-toh-rahN

monuments
mohN-ew mahN

musées
mew-zay

Touchy Subjects

If you realize that you've hurt or embarrassed the person you're talking to, you may want to apologize:

Oh, pardon! Je vois que ça ne vous plaît pas. oh pah-dohN zhuh vwah kuh sah nuh voo pleh pah
Oh, I'm sorry! I realize you don't like that.

Bon*, je vois que ça va trop loin. bohN zhuh vwah kuh sah vah troh lwaN
Well, I understand that this has gone too far.

Language Tip

The word *que* can mean both "what" and "that", as in sentences like *Je vois que tu vas bien.* (I see that you are doing fine.)

Do You Like It Here?

You may want to tell others how much you enjoy something or some place, or you may want to ask others for their impressions. You could say:

Ça te plaît ici? sah tuh pleh ee-see
Do you like it here?
sing. inform.

Ça vous plaît ici? sah voo pleh ee-see
Do you like it here?
sing. form./pl.

Oui, ça me plaît beaucoup. wee sah muh pleh boh-koo
Yes, I like it very much.

---

* When placed at the beginning of a sentence *bon* (good) is used to mean "well ..." or "now then ...".

Oui, à toi aussi? wee ah twah
oh-see

Yes, and how about you?
sing. inform.

Oui, à vous aussi? wee ah voo
oh-see

Yes, you too?
sing. form./pl.

Oui, c'est très bien! wee seh
treh bee-aN

Yes, it is very nice!

Oui, tout me plaît beaucoup ici.
wee too muh pleh
boh-koo pee-see

Yes, I like everything
here very much.

Ici, c'est mieux qu'à … [city].
ee-see say myuh kah

It's better here than in …

Ici, c'est mieux qu'en … [country].
ee-see seh myuh kahN

It's better here than in …

C'est aussi bien qu'à … [city].
seh toh-see bee-aN kah

It's as nice as …

C'est aussi bien qu'en … [country].
seh toh-see bee-aN kahN

It's as nice as …

Language Tip

If you want to compare two things use the word *que*
(as/than), as in *Il est aussi grand que moi* (He is as tall as I
am.) or *C'est mieux qu'en Angleterre* (It is better than in
England).

J'aime beaucoup … [city].
zhem boh-koo

I like … very much.

Je suis très content d'être ici. ♂
zhuh swee treh kohN-tahN
det-ruh ee-see

I'm very glad to be here.

Je suis très contente d'être ici. ♀ zhuh swee tren kohN-tahNt
det-ruh ee-see

I'm very glad to be here.

Je suis très content des … ♀
zhuh swee treh kohN-tahN day

I am very happy with the …

restaurants
res-toh-rahN

discothèques
dees-koh-tek

plages
plahzh

pistes de ski
peest duh ski

Maybe there's another place that you prefer:

Ça ne te plaît pas ici?
sah nuh tuh pleh pah zee-see

Don't you like it here?
sing. inform.

Ça ne vous plaît pas ici?
sah nuh voo pleh pah zee-see

Don't you like it here?
sing. form./pl.

Tu n'aimes pas trop ici?
tew nem pah troh pee-see

Don't you like it here as much?
sing. inform.

Vous n'aimez pas ici?
voo nem-ay pah-zee-see

Don't you like it here?
sing. form./pl.

Non, ça ne me plaît pas.
nohN sah nuh muh pleh pah

No, I don't like it.

Non, ça ne me plaît pas du tout. nohN sah nuh muh pleh pah dew too

No, I don't like it at all.

C'était mieux à … [city]. say-tay myuh ah

It was much nicer in …

C'était mieux en … [country]. say-tay myuh ahN

It was much nicer in …

Quand c'était? kahN say-tay

When was that?

C'était en … [year]. say-teh tahN

That was in …

C'était mieux en … [year]. say-tay myuh zahN

It was much nicer in …

Language Tip

Etre (to be) is an irregular verb. The imperfect form of *est* (is) is *était* (was).

Qu'est-ce que tu n'aimes pas? kes kuh tew nem pah

What is it that you don't like here? *sing. inform.*

Qu'est-ce que vous n'aimez pas? kes kuh voo nem-ay pah

What is it you don't like here? *sing. form./pl.*

A … [place], le temps était beaucoup mieux. ah … luh tahN ay-tay boh-koo myuh

The weather was much better in …

Language Tip

To talk about years and dates, check out the numbers on page 111.

If you are talking about the last century (as in 1965) you can say either *mille neuf cent* (one thousand nine-hundred) or *dix-neuf cent* (nineteen hundred). Then add the decade (for 65 this would be 60: *soixante*). To the decade, add a hyphen then the ones (for 65 it would be *soixante-cinq*). 1965 in French therefore is:

mille neuf cent soixante-cinq (meel nuhf sahN swah-sahNt-sank) or

dix-neuf cent soixante-cinq (deez-nuhf sahN swah-sahNt-sank)

For 2000, just *deux mille* (two thousand); 2005 therefore is *deux mille cinq* (duh meel sank).

In French, a year is preceded by the preposition *en* (in).

To talk about what you want to do during your trip, try these phrases:

Qu'est-ce qu'on fait?
kess kohN feh

What should we do?

C'est très bien de faire tout ça.
say treh bee-aN duh fair too sah

It's great that there's so much to do.

Je ne vais pas très tard au lit.
zhuh nuh veh pah treh tahr oh lee

I'm not going to bed very late.

**Je ne vais pas tard au lit.
Et toi?** zhuh nuh veh pah tahr oh lee eh twah

I'm not going to bed very late. And you?
sing. inform.

Non, nous n'allons pas tard au lit. Et vous? nohN noo nah-lohN pah tahr oh lee eh voo

No, we don't go to bed very late. And you? *sing. form/pl.*

Moi, je n'ai pas de temps à perdre. mwah zhuh nay pah duh tahN ah pair-druh

I really don't want to lose time.

Qu'est-ce que tu aimes faire? kes kuh tew em fair

What do you like to do? *sing. inform.*

Qu'est-ce que vous aimez faire? kes kuh voo zem-may fair

What do you like to do? *sing. form./pl.*

J'aime manger. zhem mahN-zhay

I like to eat.

J'aime faire à manger*. zhem fair ah mahN-zhay

I like to cook.

J'aime aller en ville. zhem ah-lay ahN veel

I like going to town.

J'aime faire les magasins*. zhem fair lay mah-gah-zaN

I like window shopping.

J'aime prendre le temps. zhem prahN-druh luh tahN

I like to take my time.

J'aime avoir du temps pour moi. zhem ah-vwah dew tahN poor mwah

I like to have time to myself.

---

* Idiomatic expressions:
faire à manger fair ah mahN-zhay   to cook
faire les magasins fair lay mah-gah-zaN to go window shopping

You may want to talk about the length of your trip:

Combien de temps passes-tu en tout ici? kohN-bee-aN duh tahN pahss-tew ahN too ee-see

How long are you staying here? *sing. inform.*

Combien de temps passez-vous en tout ici? kohN-bee-aN duh tahN pahs-say voo ahN too ee-see

How long are you staying here? *sing. form./pl.*

Je passe … [number] nuits. Et toi? zhuh pahss… nwee eh twah

I'm staying for … nights. And you? *sing. inform.*

Je passe …[number] nuits. Et vous? zhuh pahss… nwee eh voo

I'm staying for … nights And you? *sing. form./pl.*

Je suis arrivé ♂ … [weekday]. Et toi? zhuh swee zah-ree-veh… eh twah

I arrived on … And you? *sing. inform.*

Je suis arrivée ♀ … [weekday]. Et vous? zhuh swee zah-ree-veh… eh voo

I arrived on … And you? *sing. form./pl.*

Language Tip

The days of the week do not take a preposition in French:
I arrived on Monday. – *Je suis arrivé lundi*.
See page 112 for a complete list of the days of the week in French.

Weather

The weather is a popular and easy conversation topic. You can start by asking:

Il va faire quel temps aujourd'hui? eel vah fair kel tahN oh-zhoor-dwee	What will the weather be like today?
Il va faire quel temps demain? eel vah fair kel tahN duh maN	What will the weather be like tomorrow?
Il va faire beau*. eel vah fair boh	It will be nice.
Il fait beau aujourd'hui. eel feh boh oh-zhoor-dwee	It's nice today.
Il fait très beau. eel feh treh boh	It's very nice.
Aujourd'hui, il fait une très belle journée! oh-zhoor-dwee eel feh ewn treh bel zhoor-nay	What a wonderful day it is today!
Il fait aussi beau aux États-Unis**? eel feh oh-see boh ohzay-tah-zew-nee	Is the weather in the US nice as well?
Il va faire très beau demain aussi. eel vah fair treh boh duh-maN oh-see	Tomorrow will be another beautiful day.

---

* Idiomatic expression:
  Il fait beau. eel fait boh   It is nice.

** **en Grande-Bretagne** ahN grahNd bruh-tahn-yuh   in Great Britain
   en Canada ahN kah-nah-dah   in Canada

You may be thrilled with the rain, sun, snow or wind. Here is how to express your excitement:

J'aime bien ce temps!
zhem bee-aN suh tahN

I love this weather!

Quel beau temps! kel boh-tahN

What wonderful weather!

Unfortunately, there is no guarantee against bad weather:

Quel temps! kel tahN

What (miserable) weather!

Il ne va pas faire beau.
eel nuh vah pah fair boh

It will not be nice.

Il ne fait pas beau aujourd'hui.
eel nuh feh pah boh oh-zhoor-dwee

It's not nice today.

Il ne fait pas beau du tout!
eel nuh feh pah boh dew too

It's absolutely awful!

Je n'aime pas ce temps!
zhuh nem pah suh tahN

I don't like this weather!

Il fait plus beau aux États-Unis*?
eel feh plew boh ohzay-tah-zew-nee

Is it any better in the US?

Il ne fait pas très beau aujourd'hui, mais on fait avec**!
eel nuh feh pah treh boh oh-zhoor-dwee meh ohN feh ah-vek

It isn't very nice today, but we'll make the best of it!

---

* **en Grande-Bretagne** ahN grahNd bruh-tahn-yuh   in Great Britain
  en Canada ahN kah-nah-dah   in Canada
** Idiomatic expression:
  on fait avec ohN feh ah-vek   we'll make the best of it

Paying Compliments

Small compliments can work wonders. Try saying something nice to your new friends:

Tu le fais bien. tew luh feh bee-aN — You do that well.
sing. inform.

Vous le faites très bien.
voo luh fet bee-aN — You do that very well.
sing. form./pl.

Tu fais du mieux que tu peux.
tew feh dew myuh kuh tew puh — I can see that you are trying your best.
sing. inform.

Vous faites de votre mieux.
voo fet duh voh-truh myuh — You really try your best.
sing. form./pl.

Tu es beau aujourd'hui. ♂
ew eh boh oh-zhoor-dwee — You look handsome today.
sing. inform.

Tu es belle aujourd'hui. ♀
ew eh bel oh-zhoor-dwee — You look pretty today.
sing. inform.

Vous êtes beau. ♂ voo zet boh — You are handsome.
sing. form./pl.

Vous êtes belle. ♀ voo zet bel — You look pretty.
sing. form./pl.

Language Tip

In the formal address (*vous*) the adjective takes the singular and follows the gender of the person addressed. Consequently you can say *vous êtes beau* only to a man and *vous êtes belle* only to a woman.

Ça te va très bien.
sah vah treh bee-aN

This really suits you well.
sing. inform.

Ça vous va bien.
sah voo vah bee-aN

This suits you.
sing. form.

Ça me plaît beaucoup!
sah muh pleh boh-koo

I like this very much!

Ce … vous va bien.
suh… voo vah bee-aN

This … suits you.
sing. form.

pull
pewl

pantalon
pahN-tah-lohN

t-shirt
tee-shairt

short
shawt

Language Tip

Don't hesitate to ask for the names of things/objects unknown to you. Simply pointing at something can get someone to say the word in French. This way you will expand your vocabulary and be able to express even more.

The adjective *beau* can be used to refer to almost anything that people like to show you:

Que c'est beau! kuh seh boh   How nice!

Language Tip

If you are marveling at something, you can use the expression above and add *que* to say *Que c'est beau!* (How nice!) *Que c'est bon!* (How good!/How delicious!)

Quel beau cadeau! kel boh kah-doh	What a nice present!
C'est beau! seh boh	This is nice!
C'est très beau! seh treh boh	This is very nice!
C'est très très beau! seh treh treh boh	That looks really good!

Language Tip

Though it may look slightly odd at first sight, it is customary in French to repeat the word *très* (very) a number of times to give it emphasis: *C'est très très très beau* – "That is really, really, really nice". Where you might opt to add such words as "extremely" or "outstanding", the French just add *très* a few more times to express their enthusiasm.

C'est un très beau cadeau! seh taN treh boh kah-doh	This is really a very nice present!
C'est un très beau ...! seh taN treh boh	This is really a very nice ...!

chien
shee-aN

pull
pewl

pantalon
pahN-tah-lohN

sac à main
sahk-ah-maN

When speaking about food the word *bon* is always a good bet:

C'est un très bon repas.
seh taN treh bohN ruh-pah

This is a very good meal.

C'est une très bonne boisson.
seh tewn treh bun bwahs-sohN

This is a very good drink.

**Où peut-on acheter cette
bonne boisson?** oo puh tohN
ahsh-tay set bun
bwahs-sohN

Where can I buy this
delicious drink?

Ce repas est très bon.
suh ruh-pah eh treh bohN

This meal tastes/is
very good.

Ce … est très bon.
suh … eh treh bohN

This … tastes/is
very good.

chocolat
shoh-koh-lah

fromage
froh-mahzh

vin
vaN

croissant
kwahs-sahN

Country and Culture Tip

Though the French are known for their palate and excellent
cooking skills, they don't make a fuss over breakfast (*petit-
déjeuner*). The classic French breakfast usually consists of
a cup of coffee and a croissant. Later in the day, the French
eat a hot meal both at lunch (*déjeuner*) and at dinner (*dîner*).

Accommodations

Finding a Room

If you are looking for accommodations, ask:

J'aimerais avoir une chambre pour cette nuit.
zhem-air-ray ah-vwah ewn shahN-bruh poor set nwee

I would like to have a room for tonight.

J'ai besoin d'une chambre pour ce soir. zhay buh-zwaN dewn zhahN-bruh poor suh swah

I need a room for tonight.

Nous avons besoin d'une chambre non loin de …
noo zah-vohN buh-zwaN dewn shahN-bruh nohN lwaN duh

We need a room not far from …

J'ai besoin d'une chambre en ville. zhay buh-zwaN dewn shahn-bruh ahN veel

I need a room in town.

You may get as a response:

Je n'ai pas de chambre pour ce soir. zhuh nay pah duh shahN-bruh suh swah

I don't have a room (available) for tonight.

If so, you can reply:

Je vois, vous ne pouvez pas nous aider. zhuh vwah voo nuh poo-veh pah noo-zed-ay

I understand that you cannot help us.
sing. form./pl.

Vous avez une chambre pour nous ce soir? voo zah-veh ewn shahN-bruh poor noo suh swah

Do you still have a room for us tonight?
sing. form./pl.

Country and Culture Tip

Besides regular hotels there are other means of accommodation that are listed in the French *office de tourisme* (tourist information center). These include, among others, *chambres d'hôtel* (guest rooms), which are offered by private households and often include breakfast and dinner as well.

A *gîte* is a furnished vacation appartment.

When *camping à la ferme,* you can pitch your tent on a farmer's property.

To enjoy your vacation, make sure you compare rooms and prices:

Une chambre pas trop chère, s'il vous plaît! ewn shahN-bruh pah troh shair seel voo pleh
A room that is not too expensive, please!

J'ai besoin d'une chambre pas très chère. zhay buh-zwaN dewn shahN-bruh pah treh shair
I need a room that is not too expensive.

La chambre peut faire au plus ... € (euro). lluh shahN-bruh puh fair oh plewss ... uhroh
The room must not cost more than ... €.

La nuit peut faire au plus ... € (euro). lah nwee puh fair oh plewss ... uhroh
The room should not be more than ... € per night.

See page 111 for numbers.

At the Reception

If you have made reservations in advance:

La chambre pour … [your name], s'il vous plaît. lah shahN-bruh poor … seel voo pleh
The room for …, please.

Vous avez une chambre pour moi. voo zah-veh ewn shahN-bruh poor mwah
You have a room reserved in my name. *sing. form./pl.*

Quelle est la chambre pour nous? kel eh lah shahN-bruh poor noo
Which one is our room?

If you don't have reservations, describe to the receptionist exactly what you are looking for:

Nous aimerions avoir une chambre avec un grand lit, s'il vous plaît. noo zem-air-ee-ohN ah-vwah ewn shahN-bruh ah-vek aN grahN lee seel voo pleh
We would like a double room, please.

Nous aimerions avoir une grande chambre avec un grand lit. noo zem-air-ee-ohN ah-vwah ewn grahNd shahN-bruh ah-vek aN grahN lee
We would like a large double room.

Nous aimerions avoir une petite chambre avec un grand lit. noo zem-air-ee-ohN ah-vwah ewn puh-teet shahN-bruh ah-vek aN grahN lee
We would like a small double room.

Est-ce que les lits sont grands? ess kuh lay lee sohN grahN
Are the beds large?

Nous avons besoin de deux lits.
noo zah-vohN buh-zwaN duh duh lee

We need separate beds.

**Bon, nous prenons une chambre
avec deux lits.** bohN noo pruh-nohN
ewn shahN-bruh ah-vek duh lee

OK, we'll take a room
with two separate beds.

**Une grande chambre avec un
grand lit pour nous et un petit
lit pour le petit, s'il vous plaît.**
ewn grahNd shahN-bruh ah-vek aN
grahN lee poor noo eh an puh-tee
lee poor luh puh-tee seel voo pleh

A large double room with
a small bed for the
child, please.

**Nous avons besoin de deux
chambres.**
noo zah-vohN buh-zwaN duh
duh shahN-bruh

We need two rooms.

Country and Culture Tip

The bigger rooms in French hotels generally have one king
size bed. If you want two separate beds ask for *lits jumeaux*,
two twin beds.

And how long do you intend to stay?

**Pour combien de nuits, s'il vous
plaît?** poor kohN-bee-aN duh
nwee seel voo pleh

For how many nights?

Quand arrivez-vous?
kahN ah-ree-veh-voo

When will you arrive?
sing. form./pl.

Nous avons besoin des chambres pour une nuit. noo zah-vohN buh-zwaN day shahN-bruh poor ewn nwee

We would like the rooms for one night.

On peut avoir la chambre pour une nuit? ohN puh tah-vwah lah shahN-bruh poor ewn nwee

Can we have the room just for one night?

Nous allons passer deux nuits ici. noo zah-lohN pahs-say duh nwee zee-see

We will stay here for two nights.

Nous passons … nuits ici. noo pahs-sohn … nwee zee-see

We spend … nights here.

See page 111 for numbers.

Furnishing and Extras

If you want to know more about the rooms or have specific requests, ask these questions:

Combien de chambres avez-vous en tout*? kohN-bee-aN duh shahN-bruh ah-veh voo ahN too

How many rooms in total do you have? *sing. form./pl.*

Pouvons-nous avoir une très belle chambre? poo-vohN noo zah-vah ewn treh bel shahN-bruh

Could we have a very nice room?

---

* Idiomatic expression:
  en tout ahN too

in all/total/all together

Nous aimerions avoir la plus belle chambre. noo zem-air-ee-ohN ah-vwah lah bel shahN-bruh

We would like to have the nicest room.

Nous avons besoin d'une plus grande chambre. noo zah-vohN buh-zwaN dewn plew grahNd shahN-bruh

We need a larger room.

Quelle est la chambre la mieux que vous avez? kel eh lah shahN-bruh lah myuh kuh voo zah-veh

Which is the best room you have?
sing. form./pl.

Language Tip

In the example above, the word *que* is a pronoun. It is always positioned after the noun it relates to.

Que peut-on voir de la chambre? kuh puh-tohN vwah duh lah shahN-bruh

What can we see from our room?

Nous aimerions voir de la chambre la ... noo zem-air-ee-ohN vwah duh lah shahN-bruh lah

We would like to see the ... from our room.

mer
mair

plage
plahzh

montagne
mohN-tahn-yuh

rivière
reev-yair

A
C
C
O
M
M
O
D
A
T
I
O
N
S

La chambre est avec …?
ah shahN-bruh et ah-vek

Does the room have
a … ?

douche
doosh

baignoire
ben-wahr

WC
veh say

télé
tay-lay

Country and Culture Tip

Cabinet de toilette designates a small bathroom that might include a sink and often a shower or a toilet as well. It is separated from the rest of the room by a partition. If you want a room that includes a *cabinet de toilette* be sure to ask if it's included in the price.

If you want to take a look at the room, ask:

**Peut-on voir la chambre,
s'il vous plaît?** puh tohN vwah
lah shahN-bruh seel voo pleh

Can we see the room,
please?

**J'aimerais voir la chambre, s'il
vous plaît.** zhem-air-ay vwah lah
shahN-bruh seel voo pleh

I'd like to see the room,
please.

**Vous pouvez nous faire voir
les chambres, s'il vous plaît?**
voo poo-veh noo fair vwah lay
shahN-bruh seel voo pleh

Can you show us the
rooms, please?
sing. form./pl.

La chambre est déjà faite?
lah shahN-bruh eh day-zhah fet

Is the room ready already?

If the room is not quite what you expected, you could say:

Cette chambre est beaucoup trop grande pour moi.
set shahN-bruh eh boh-koo troh grahNd poor mwah

This room is far too large for me.

Avez-vous une plus petite chambre? ah-veh voo ewn plew puh-teet shahN-bruh

Do you have a smaller room? *sing. form./pl.*

Cette chambre est trop petite pour nous. set shahN-bruh eh troh puh-teet poor noo

This room is too small for us.

Avez-vous une plus grande chambre? ah-veh voo ewn plew grahNd shahN-bruh

Do you have a larger room? *sing. form./pl.*

Vous n'avez pas de chambres mieux? voo nah-veh pah duh shahN-bruh myuh

Don't you have better rooms? *sing. form./pl.*

Ask about meals at the hotel:

Nous pouvons prendre les repas ici aussi?
noo poo-vohN praN-druh lay ruh-pah ee-see oh-see

Can we also eat here?

Les repas sont en plus*?
lay ruh-pah sohN tahN plewss

Are the meals extra?

---

* Idiomatic expression:
sont en plus sohN-tahN plewss

to cost extra

Combien fait un repas?
kohN-bee-aN feh aN ruh-pah

How much is a meal?

A quelle heure sont les repas?
ah kel uhr sohn lay ruh-pah

What are the meal times?

Quand pouvons-nous prendre les repas? kahN poo-vohN noo prahN-druh lay ruh-pah

When are the meals served?

Où prenons-nous les repas?
oo pruh-nohN noo lay ruh-pah

Where do we eat our meals?

Où pouvons-nous avoir un repas à cette heure? oo poo-vohN-noo zah-vwah aN ruh-pah ah set uhr

Where can we get something to eat at this time?

The receptionist may respond:

A quelle heure aimeriez-vous manger? ah kel uhr em-air-ee-ay voo mahN-zhay

At what time would you like to eat? *sing. form./pl.*

Vous pouvez prendre votre repas à … [time]. voo poo-veh prahN-druh voh-truh ruh-pah ah

You can have your meal at … *sing. form./pl.*

And you can say:

A quelle heure mangez-vous le soir? ah kel uhr mahN-zhay-voo luh swah

At what time do you usually have dinner? *sing. form./pl.*

Nous aimerions manger à … [time]. noo zem-air-ee-ohN mahN-zhay ah

We would like to eat at …

Je mange à … [time].
zhuh mahNzh ah

I eat at …

Au plus tard à … [time].
oh plew tahr ah

At … at the latest.

**Aux États-Unis*, on ne mange
pas tard.** ohzay-tah-zew-nee
ohN nuh mahNzh pah tahr

One doesn't eat late
in the United States.

**Ici, vous mangez beaucoup plus
tard le soir.** ee-see voo mahN-zhay
boh-koo plew tahr luh swah

Here one eats dinner
much later. *sing. form./pl.*

Language Tip

In France, the 24-hour clock is often used, especially when
talking about opening and closing times.

7:00	*sept heures* (set uhr)	
7:05	*sept heures cinq* (set uhr sank)	
7:15	*sept heures et quart* (set uhr eh kahr)	
7:25	*sept heures vingt-cinq* (set uhr vaN sank)	
7:30	*sept heures et demie* (set uhr eh duh-mee)	

Note:

7:40   *huit heures moins vingt* (weet uhr mwaN vaN)
        [literally 8 minus 20]

7:45   *huit heures moins le quart* (weet uhr mwaN luh kahr)
        [literally 8 minus a quarter]

7:55   *huit heures moins cinq* (weet uhr mwaN sank)
        [literally 8 minus 5]

Noon is called *midi* , midnight *minuit*. *Du matin*, is "am", *du
soir* is "pm".

---

* **en Grande-Bretagne** ahN grahNd bruh-tahn-yuh   in Great Britain
   en Canada ahN kah-nah-dah   in Canada

See page 111 page for numbers.

You might want to go for a drink:

Où pouvons nous avoir une boisson à cette heure? oo poo-vohN noo zah-vwah ewn bwahs-sohN ah set uhr

Where can we get a drink at this time?

Pouvons-nous avoir quelque chose à boire ici? poo-vohN noo zah-vwah kel-kuh shohz ah bwah ee-see

Can we get something to drink here?

Quelle boisson aimeriez-vous avoir? kel bwahs-sohN em-air-ee-ay-voo zah-vwah

What kind of drink would you like? *sing. form./pl.*

Quelle boisson aimes-tu le plus? kel bwahs-sohN em-tew luh plewss

What kind of drink do you like best? *sing. inform.*

Quelle boisson aimez-vous le plus? kel bwahs-sohN em-ay voo luh plewss

What kind of drink do you like best? *sing. form./pl.*

Oh pardon, c'est votre boisson! oh pah-dohN seh voh-truh bwahs-sohN

Oh, excuse me, that's your drink! *sing. form./pl.*

Pardon, mais ce n'est pas votre boisson! pah-dohN meh suh neh pah voh-truh bwahs-sohN

Excuse me, but this is not your drink! *sing. form./pl.*

Pardon, mais je n'ai pas de boisson. pah-dohN meh zhuh nay pah duh bwahs-sohN

Excuse me, but I don't have a drink yet.

Pardon, mais je n'ai rien à boire.
pah-dohN meh zhuh nay ree-aN
ah bwah

Excuse me, but I don't have anything to drink yet.

Prices

To inquire about the price of the room and the extras, ask:

Combien fait la chambre?
kohN-bee-aN feh lah shahN-bruh

How much does the room cost?

Combien fait une nuit?
kohN-bee-aN feh ewn nwee

How much is it per night?

Et combien font deux nuits?
eh kohN-bee-aN fohN duh nwee

And how much is it for two nights?

Combien font les boissons en chambre? kohN-bee-aN fohN lay bwahs-sohN ahN shahN-bruh

How much do the drinks in my room cost?

Combien ça fait quand on appelle de la chambre?
kohN-bee-aN sah feh kahN tohN nah-pel duh lah shahN-bruh

How much does a phone call from my room cost?

Deciding

If you have found what you are looking for, say:

La chambre me plaît beaucoup.
llah shahN-bruh muh pleh boh-koo

I like the room very much.

Nous la prenons. noo lah pruh-nohN We'll take it.

Je peux prendre cette chambre?
zhuh puh prahN-druh set shahN-bruh

Can I get this room?

Nous aimerions prendre cette chambre. noo zem-air-ee-ohN prahN-druh set shahN-bruh

We would like to take this room.

Alternatively you may want to continue searching:

C'est cher. seh shair

That is too expensive.

C'est très très cher! seh treh treh shair

That is very, very expensive!

C'est trop cher pour nous! seh troh shair poor noo

That is too expensive for us!

C'est beaucoup trop cher! seh boh-koo troh shair

That is far too expensive!

La chambre est très belle, mais elle est trop chère pour nous. ah shahN-bruh eh treh bel meh el eh troh shair poor noo

The room is very nice, but it is too expensive for us.

Merci, mais la chambre ne me plaît pas du tout. mair-see meh lah shahN-bruh nuh muh pleh pah dew too

Thanks, but I don't like that room at all.

Merci, mais la chambre n'est pas très belle. mair-see meh lah shahN-bruh neh pah treh bel

Thanks, but the room is not very nice.

Merci, mais nous ne prenons pas la chambre. mair-see meh noo nuh pruh-nohN pah lah shahN-bruh

Thanks, but we will not take the room.

Merci de nous faire voir les chambres. mair-see duh noo fair vwah lay shahN-bruh

Thank you for showing us the rooms.

Service

In case someone is calling you on the phone:

Pardon, on vous appelle.
pah-dohN ohN voo zah-pel

Excuse me, I have a call here for you. *sing. form./pl.*

Oui, je le prends.
wee zhuh luh prahN

Yes, I'll take it.

On vous a appelé des États-Unis* aujourd'hui. ohN voo zah ah-play day-zay-tah-zew-nee oh-zhoor-dwee

There was a call from the US for you today. *sing. form./pl.*

And if you need a wake-up call in the morning, ask:

Vous pouvez nous appeler à … [time], s'il vous plaît? voo poo-veh noo zah-play ah … seel voo pleh

Could you please give us a call at …? *sing. form./pl.*

A quelle heure je peux vous appeler? ah kel uhr zhuh puh voo zah-play

At what time shall I give you a wake-up call? *sing. form./pl.*

A quelle heure pouvons-nous vous appeler? ah kel uhr poo-vohN noo voo zah-play

At what time shall we give you a call? *sing. form./pl.*

Appelez-moi à … [time]!
ah-play-mwah ah

Call me at …!

A … [time], s'il vous plaît!
ah … seel voo pleh

At …, please! *sing. form./pl.*

---

* **de Grande-Bretagne** duh grahNd bruh-tahn-yuh from Great Britain
de Canada dew kah-nah-dah from Canada

See page 111 for numbers.

If there is anything else you need:

Nous avons besoin d'un lit en plus. noo zah-vohN buh-zwaN daN lee ahn plewss

We would need an extra bed.

Nous avons besoin d'un … en plus. noo zah-vohN buh-zwaN daN … ahn plewss

We would need an extra …

sèche-cheveux
sesh-shuh-vuh

cintre
saN-truh

savon
sah-vohN

Où est-ce que je peux avoir des …? oo ess kuh zhuh puh ah-vwah day

Where can I find a …?

Je peux avoir des …, s'il vous plaît? zhu puh ah-vwah day … seel voo pleh

Could I have …, please?

pellicules
pel-ih-kewl

piles
peel

cartes postales
kaht paws-tahl

allumettes
ah-lew-met

Complaints

Should you need to complain about your neighbor:

Pouvez-vous aller voir dans la chambre ... [room number]?
poo-veh voo ah-lay vwah dahN lah shahN-bruh

Could you please check on room number ...?
sing. form./pl.

Ça ne peut plus faire*!
sah nuh puh plew fair

It can't go on like that!

Je n'en peux plus!
zhuh nahN puh plew

I can't take this any more!

Il est très tard et nous aimerions aller au lit! eel eh treh tahr eh noo zem-air-ee-ohN ah-lay oh lee

It is very late and we want to go to bed!

Il est temps de faire quelque chose. eel eh tahN duh fair kel-kuh shohz

It is time to do something about this.

Il n'a rien de mieux à faire à cette heure? eel nah ree-aN duh myuh ah fair ah set uhr

Hasn't he got anything better to do at this time?

Je ne suis pas content de la chambre. ♂ zhuh nuh swee pah kohN-tahN duh lah shahN-bruh

I am not happy with this room.

---

* The expression *peut faire* has two meanings. One can translate it literally with "can do" as in *Il peut le faire.* (He can do it.), but also as an idiomatic expression *Ça ne peut plus faire!* (It can't go on like this!).

Je ne suis pas contente de la chambre. ♀ zhuh nuh swee pah kohN-tahNt duh lah shahN-bruh

I am not happy with this room.

If your room isn't ready, you can say:

Nous aimerions aller dans la chambre, mais elle n'est pas faite. Noo zem-air-ee-ohN ah-lay dahn lah shahN-bruh meh el neh pah fet

We would like to go to our room, but it isn't ready yet.

Nous n'avons pas beaucoup de temps aujourd'hui. noo nah-vohN pah boh-koo duh tahN oh-zhoor-dwee

We don't have much time today.

Pouvez-vous faire la chambre, s'il vous plaît. poo-veh voo fair lah shahN-bruh seel voo pleh

Could you please get our room ready now. *sing. form./pl.*

Comment? La chambre n'est pas faite? koN-maN lah shahN-bruh neh pah

I beg your pardon? The room is not ready yet?

Vacation Activities

Getting There

Wherever you go during your vacation, sooner or later you'll need to ask for directions:

Où vas-tu? oo vah tew

Where do you go?
sing. inform.

Où allez-vous? oo ah-lay voo

Where do you go?
sing. form./pl.

Je vais en ville.
zhuh veh zahN veel

I'm going into town.

J'aimerais aller à … [destination].
zhem-air-ay ah-lay ah

I'd like to go to …

Où c'est? oo seh

Where is that?

C'est ici … [destination]?
set ee-see

Is this …?

Non, ce n'est pas ici!
nohN suh neh pah zee-see

No, that's not here!

Pardon, c'est bien ici …?
pah-dohN seh byaN ee-see

Excuse me, is this here …?

Ce n'est pas très loin d'ici, non?
suh neh pah treh lwaN dee-see
nohN

It is not far from here, is it?

Ce n'est pas trop loin?
suh neh pah troh lwaN

It is not too far?

Est-ce que c'est loin d'ici?
ess kuh seh lwaN dee-see

Is it far from here?

C'est trop loin. seh troh lwaN

That's too far.

Comment pouvons-nous y aller?
kohN-mohN poo-vohN-noo
zee ah-lay

How can we get there?

Comment pouvons-nous aller a ... ? kohN-mohN poo-vohN
noo zah-lay ah

How can we get to ...?

If you are traveling by public transportation, you could ask one of the following questions:

Pouvons-nous prendre le ... ?
poo-vohN noo prahN-druh luh

Can we take the ... ?

Où pouvons-nous prendre le ... ? oo poo-vohN-noo
prahN-druh luh

Where can we get the ... ?

Quand passe le ... ? kahN
pahss luh

When will the ... leave?

A quelle heure arrive le ... ?
ah kel uhr ah-reev luh

At what time does the ... arrive?

Où va le ... ? oo vah luh

Where does the ... go?

A quelle heure ouvre le ... ?
ah kel uhr oo-vruh luh

At what time does the first ... leave?

A quelle heure est ce qu'il n'y a plus de ... ? ah kel uhr eh
suh keel nee-ah plew duh

At what time does the ... service stop?

Quel ... pouvons-nous prendre?
kel ... poo-vohN-noo prahN-druh

Which... can we take?

**Vous pouvez prendre le ... pour
aller à ...** voo poo-vay prahN-druh
luh ... poor ah-lay ah

You can take the ...
to ... *sing. form./pl.*

bus	**métro**	**train**	**tram**
bewss	may-troh	traN	trahm

Est-il à l'heure? eh-teel ah luhr

Will it be on time?

Il va arriver. eel vah ah-ree-veh

It is about to arrive.

Il est déjà arrivé.
eel eh day-zhah ah-ree-veh

It has already arrived.

**Combien ça fait pour aller
en ville?** kohN-byaN
sah feh poor ah-lay ahN veel

How much is the fare
into town?

Shopping

**Aujourd'hui, je vais faire les
magasins*.** oh-zhoor-dwee
zhuh veh fair lay mah-gah-zaN

I'm going window
shopping today.

**J'aimerais aller faire les
magasins demain.**
zhem-air-ay ah-lay fair layy
mah-gah-zaN

I'd like to go window
shopping tomorrow.

---

* Idiomatic expression:
   faire les magasins fair lay mah-gah-zaN to go window shopping

Vous pouvez me dire où est le magasin de …? voo poo-vaz muh deer oo eh luh mah-gah-zaN duh

Could you please tell me where I can find a … shop? *sing. form./pl.*

vêtements
vet-mahN

journaux
zjoor-noh

fleurs
fluhr

vélos
vay-loh

chaussures
shoh-sewr

cigarettes
see-gah-ret

fruits et légumes
frewee eh lay-gewm

poissons
pwahsohN

If you want to know the opening hours of a shop or store:

Quand êtes-vous ouvert? kahN et voo zoo-vair

When are you open? *sing. form./pl.*

Le magasin est ouvert de … [time] à … [time]. luh mah-gah-zaN eh too-vair duh… ah

Our shop is open from … until …

A quelle heure ouvre le magasin? ah kel uhr oo-vruh luh mah-gah-zaN

At what time do you open?

A quelle heure est-ce qu'il n'est plus ouvert? ah kel uhr ess keel neh plew zoo-vair

At what time do you close?

Vous êtes ouvert … [day of the week]? voos zet oo-vair

Are you open on … ? *sing. form./pl.*

See pages 111–112 for numbers and days of the week.

Country and Culture Tip

When you want to go shopping keep in mind that most shops in France are closed on Monday morning. They will be open all day Saturday, often as late as 7:30 pm.

Outside of Paris many of the smaller shops and stores will close for a two-hour lunch break. This does not generally apply to shopping centers and supermarkets, which are open throughout the day. You will find that there can be significant differences in the opening hours between urban centers like Paris and rural areas.

Let's go shopping for clothes. First, let's talk about sizes:

Quelle taille faites-vous?
kel tigh-yuh fet voo

What size are you?
sing. form./pl.

De quelle taille avez-vous besoin? duh kel tigh-yuh ah-vay voo buh-zwaN

What size do you need? *sing. form./pl.*

C'est quelle taille, s'il vous plaît?
seh kel tigh-yuh seel voo pleh

What size is this, please?

J'ai besoin du … [size].
zhay buh-zwaN dew

I need size …

Je fais du … [size]. zhuh feh dew

I have size …

Nous n'avons que du … [size]. noo nah-vohN kuh dew

We have only size …

Language Tip
The last example on the previous page applies the negative clause *ne … que* (only), as in *Nous n'avons que du …* (We have only size …)

Vous l'avez aussi en … [size]?
voo lah-vay oh-see ahN

Do you have this also in size …? *sing. form./pl.*

See page 111 for numbers.

Cette taille ne vous va pas mieux? set tigh-yuh nuh voo vah pah myuh

This size doesn't fit you better? *sing. form./pl.*

Bon, on va voir.
bohN ohN vah vwah

Well, let's see.

On va voir ça! ohN vah vwah sah

We'll see in a minute!

Non, ce n'est pas la bonne taille.
nohN suh neh pah lah bun tigh-yuh

No, that's not my size.

Oui, c'est la bonne taille.
wee seh lah bun tigh-yuh

Yes, that's the right size.

Non, c'est trop grand pour moi.
nohN seh troh grahN poor mwah

No, that's too large for me.

Non, c'est trop petit.
nohN seh troh puh-tee

No, that's too small.

Vous n'avez pas une taille plus petite? voo nah-vay pah zewn tigh-yuh plew puh-teet

Do you have this in a smaller size? *sing. form./pl.*

Vous n'avez pas une taille plus grande? voo nah-vay pah zewn tigh-yuh plew grahNd

Do you have this also in a larger size? *sing. form./pl.*

Country and Culture Tip

France is known throughout the world for its famous fashion designers such as Christian Dior, Coco Chanel, Yves Saint-Laurent, Jean-Paul Gaultier, Christian Lacroix, etc., whose *prêt-à-porter* collections (ready-to-wear collections) are often available in larger department stores these days.

French sizes differ from those specified in the US and the UK. A French size 36 would be a size 8/10 in the US or a size 30/32 in the UK.

Next you will want to find the right clothes:

Ça me va bien. sah muh vah byaN

This suits/fits me.

Ça vous va très bien. sah voo vah treh byaN

This really suits/fits you. *sing. form./pl.*

Et ça, ça ne me va pas mieux? eh sah sah nuh muh vah pah myuh

Doesn't this fit me better?

Mais ça me va! meh sah muh vah

But this suits/fits me!

Ça me va bien. sah muh vah byaN

This suits/fits me.

J'aimerais l'acheter. zhem-air-ay lahsh-tay

I'd like to buy it.

C'est très beau! seh treh boh

This is wonderful!

Je vais l'acheter.
zhuh veh lahsh-tay

I'll buy it right away.

C'est ça que j'aime!
seh sah kuh zhem

That's just what I love!

C'est ça que j'aimerais m'acheter.
seh sah kuh zhem-air-ay mahsh-tay

That's just what I want
to buy (for myself)!

C'est un très beau magasin!
seh taN treh boh mah-gah-zaN

This is a very nice shop!

**Merci, mais ça ne me va pas du
tout.** mair-see meh sah nuh
muh vah pah dew too

Thank you, but this doesn't
suit/fit me at all.

Merci, mais je ne le prends pas.
mair-see meh zhuh nuh luh
prahN pah

Thank you, but I will
not take it.

If you want to buy a typical French souvenir to take back home
for your friends or relatives:

J'aimerais acheter un cadeau.
zhem-air-ay ahsh-tay aN kah-doh

I would like to buy
a present.

Nous allons acheter un cadeau.
noo zah-lohN ahsh-tay aN kah-doh

We will go to buy
a present.

C'est d'ici? seh dee-see

Is this from around here?

**J'ai besoin d'un beau cadeau pas
trop cher.** zhay buh-zwaN daN
boh kah-doh pah troh shair

I need a nice present that
is not too expensive.

Le cadeau peut faire plus.
luh kah-doh puh fair plewss

If the present costs a bit
more, that's OK.

Country and Culture Tip

Typical souvenirs to take home from France would be cheeses, mustard, wine and liqueur as well as local specialties from one of the many markets (herbs, garments, soap). Check with customs for restrictions, especially if you want to bring back food items.

Another obvious choice would be fragrances or clothing items from a designer French label but these would be very expensive gifts!

Entertainment

On va au …? ohN vah oh

Shall we go to the …?

J'aimerais aller au …
zhem-air-ay ah-lay oh

I'd like to go to the …

cinéma
see-nay-mah

théâtre
tay-ah-truh

musée
mew-zay

casino
kah-zee-noh

Oui, moi aussi.
wee mwah oh-seei

Yes, me too.

Non, je n'aime pas ça!
nohN zhuh nem pah sah

No, I don't like that!

C'est à quelle heure?
seh ah kel uhr

At what time does it start?

C'est où? seh oo	Where does it take place?
Combien ça fait pour un? kohN-byaN sah feh poor aN	How much does it cost per person?
Combien ça fait pour deux? kohN-byaN sah feh poor duh	How much does it cost for two?

Country and Culture Tip

In most French cities you can find papers that list theater performances, films and museum exhibitions. Also included is a directory of restaurants and cafés. Check out one of the local newsstands or tourist offices to obtain a free copy. In Paris, look for *L'Officiel des spectacles* and *Pariscope*.

Leisure and Sports

If you want some extra excitement during your vacation, try out a new sport:

Aujourd'hui, j'aimerais faire quelque chose de bien. oh-zhoor-dwee zhem-air-ay fair kel-kuh shohz duh byaN	Today, I want to do something special/great.
Je suis content de pouvoir le faire. ♂ zhuh swee kohN-tahN duh poo-vwah luh fair	I'd be happy to try this.
Je suis contente de pouvoir le faire. ♀ zhuh swee kohN-tahNt duh poo-vwah luh fair	I'd be happy to try this.

Tu fais de la ...?
tew feh duh lah

Do you do ...? *sing. inform.*

Vous faites de la ...?
voo fet duh lah

Do you do ...?
sing. form./pl.

J'aimerais faire de la ...
zhem-air-ay fair duh lah

I would like to go ...

randonnée
rahN-dun-nay

plongée
plohN-zhay

voile
vwahl

barque
bahk

Language Tip

In French, many activities such as hiking, walking, diving, sailing or rowing are expressed by using the noun together with *faire de* , e.g., *faire de voile* (sailing).

J'en ai déjà fait. Et toi?
zhahN neh day-zhah feh. eh twah

I've done this before.
And you? *sing. inform.*

Non, je n'en ai pas fait.
nohN zhuh nahN eh pah feh

No, I've not tried this yet.

Language Tip

En is used in a variety of different functions in French and can be translated in numerous ways. In the last expression, it means "this".

C'était bien! say-tay byaN

That was nice!

C'était très bien!
say-tay treh byaN

That was great!

C'était très très bien!
say-tay treh treh byaN

That was fantastic!

Country and Culture Tip

One popular sport that is popular above all in the south of France is *boules* or *pétanque*, a game played by throwing balls at a stationary target. Often played on public squares or parks, this ball game has come to fulfill an important social function. Players and on-lookers freely comment on any throw.

If you know the rules you'll surely be invited to play along even if your French is not fully up to it yet!

Going Out for a Meal

If you want to go out for a meal you will have to decide what and how much you want to eat:

Qu'aimeriez-vous manger?
kem-air-ee-ay-voo mahN-zjay

What would you like to eat? *sing. form./pl.*

J'aimerais avoir des ..., s'il vous plaît. zhem-air-ay ah-vwah day ... seel voo pleh

I'd like to have ..., please.

crevettes
kray-vet

huîtres
wee-truh

escargots
es-kah-goh

tomates
toh-maht

Je prends du ... avec des ..., s'il vous plaît. zhuh prahN dew ... ah-vek day... seel voo pleh

I'll have ... with ..., please.

poisson
pwahs-sohN

porc
pawr

poulet
poo-lay

canard
kah-nah

petits pois
puh-tee pwah

pommes de terre
pum duh tair

frites
freet

haricots
ah-ree-koh

J'aimerais aussi une ..., s'il vous plaît. zhem-air-ay oh-see ewn ... seel voo pleh

I'd also like ... please.

glace
glahss

mousse au chocolat
mooss oh shoh-koh-lah

part de gâteau
pahr duh gah-toh

Country and Culture Tip

A typical French meal will include at least three courses. Before dessert, a cheese platter (*un plateau de fromage*) is served to round off the main courses. The cheese platter offers between four to five different variations of cheese. It is polite, though, not to try more than two or three different types.

When eating out in a restaurant you will normally be served tap water. If this is not the case order a pitcher of water (*une carafe d'eau*). The same applies to bread (*pain*), which is also included in the price of the meal.

Tu ne manges pas?
tew nuh mahNzh pah

You're not eating anything?
sing. inform.

Vous ne mangez plus?
voo nuh mahN-zhay plew

You finished eating?
sing. form./pl.

Je ne mange pas beaucoup.
zhuh nuh mahNzh pah boh-coo

I don't eat very much.

Non merci, je ne peux plus rien manger. nohN mair-see zhuh nuh puh plew ryaN mahN-zhay

No thanks, I can't eat any more.

Je peux en avoir plus, s'il vous plaît? zhuh puh zahN ah-vwah plewss seel noo pleh

Can I have some more of that, please?

Language Tip

As already pointed out before, the preposition *en* has a number of different functions in French. Above it is used as a pronoun for the direct object, which designates a quantity: *Je peux avoir de la glace?* (Can I have ice cream?) becomes *Je peux en avoir?* (Can I have some of it?)

Surely you will also want something to drink:

Vous prenez quelque chose?
voo pruh-nay kel-kuh shohz

What can I bring you?
sing. form./pl.

Et qu'aimeriez-vous boire?
eh kem-air-ee-ay-voo bwah

And what would you like to drink? *sing. form./pl.*

J'aimerais avoir un ..., s'il vous plaît. hem-air-ay zah-vwah aN... seel voo pleh

I would like a ..., please.

verre d'eau
vair doh

jus de fruit
jew duh frewee

verre de vin rouge
vair duh vaN roozh

cocktail
kawk-tail

Tu ne bois pas? tew nuh bwah pah

You're not drinking anything?
sing. inform.

Vous ne buvez pas?
voo ne bew-vay pah

Aren't you drinking anything? *sing. form./pl.*

Tu ne prends rien?
tew nuh prahN ryaN

Don't you want anything to drink? *sing. inform.*

Vous ne prenez rien?
voo nuh pruh-nay ryaN

Don't you want to drink anything? *sing. form./pl.*

Non merci, je ne bois pas.
nohN mair-see zhuh nuh bwah pah

No thanks, I am not drinking anything.

Je ne bois plus rien ce soir.
zhuh nuh bwah plew ryaN
suh swah

I'm not drinking anymore tonight.

J'ai trop bu. zhayh troh bew

I've drunk too much.

J'ai déjà trop bu.
zhay day-zhah troh bew

I've already drunk too much.

Country and Culture Tip

The French toast one another with *Tchin-tchin!* (Cheers!) or *Santé!* (To your health!) To say "Bless you" to someone who has sneezed, use the informal expression *A tes souhaits!* or the formal *A vos souhaits!* The literal translation of this would be "As you wish!"

If you have reason to complain in a restaurant, say:

Pardon, mais ce n'est pas bon.
pah-dohN meh suh neh pah bohN

Excuse me, but this is not good.

Mais je ne peux pas le manger.
meh zhuh nuh puh pah luh mahn-zhay

But I cannot eat this.

Je ne peux pas le boire.
zhuh nuh puh pah luh bwah

I cannot drink this.

Je ne suis pas content du repas. ♂ zhuh nuh swee pah kohN-tahN dew ruh-pah

I am not satisfied with this meal.

Je ne suis pas contente du repas. ♀ zhuh nuh swee pah kohN-tahNt dew ruh-pah

I am not satisfied with this meal.

Je vous dis que je ne prends pas ce repas! zhuh voo dee kuh zhuh nuh prahN pah suh ruh-pah

I'm telling you that I don't want this dish!
sing. form./pl.

Mais le repas était trop cher.
meh luh ruh-pah ay-tay troh shair

But the meal was too expensive.

La boisson était trop chère.
ah bwahs-sohN ay-tay troh shair

The drink was too expensive.

Flirting

When you make new friends on your vacation or have a romantic encounter:

Tu as le temps ce soir?
tew ah luh tahN suh swah

Do you have time tonight?
sing. inform.

Vous avez du temps pour moi aujourd'hui? voo zah-vay dew tahN poor mwah oh-zhoor-dwee

Do you have time for me today? *sing. form./pl.*

Oui, j'ai le temps. wee zhay luh tahN

Yes, I have time.

On peut se voir demain? ohN puh suh vwah duh-maN

Will we see each other tomorrow?

If your mutual affection is growing:

Je suis très content d'être avec toi. ♂ zhuh swee treh kohN-tahN det-ruh ah-vek twah

I am very happy to be with you. *sing. inform.*

Je suis très contente d'être avec toi. ♀ zhuh swee treh kohN-tahNt det-ruh ah-vek twah

I am very happy to be with you. *sing. inform.*

C'est bien de passer du temps avec toi. seh byaN duh pahs-say dew tahN ah-vek twah

It is nice to spend time with you. *sing. inform.*

Que le temps passe! kuh luh tahN pahss

Time flies!

Tu me plais beaucoup. tew muh pleh boh-coo

You are my type. *sing. inform.*

Je t'aime bien. zhuh tem byaN

I like you very much. *sing. inform.*

Je t'aime. zhuh tem

I love you. *sing. inform.*

J'aime bien être avec toi.
zhem byaN et-ruh ah-vek twah

I love being with you.
sing. inform.

J'aimerais passer la journée avec toi. zhem-air-ay pahs-say lah zhoor-nay ah-vek twah

I want to spend the day with you.
sing. inform.

If, however, you have to resist stormy invitations or approaches, make it clear by saying:

J'ai mieux à faire! zhay myhuh ah fair

I have better things to do!

Tu n'as rien de mieux à faire?
tew nah ryaN duh myuh ah fair

Don't you have anything better to do? *sing. inform.*

Vous n'avez rien de mieux à faire? voo nah-vay ryaN duh myuh ah fair

Don't you have anything better to do?
sing. form./pl.

Je n'ai pas le temps.
zhuh nay pah luh tahN

I have no time.

Je n'ai pas besoin de toi.
zhuh nay pah buh-zwaN duh twah

I really don't need you.
sing. inform.

Je n'ai pas besoin de vous.
zhuh nay pah buh-zwaN duh voo

I really don't need you. *sing. form./pl.*

Mais tu vois bien que ça ne me plaît pas! meh tew vwah byaN kuh sah nuh muh pleh pah

But you can clearly see that I don't like this!
sing. inform.

Vous voyez bien que ça ne me plaît pas du tout! voo vwah-yay byaN kuh sah nuh muh pleh pah dew too

You can clearly see that I don't like this at all!
sing. form./pl.

Je n'ai plus rien à dire!
zhuh nay plew ryaN nah deer

I have nothing more
to say!

Language Tip

The negative in French is formed by the conjugated verb
with *ne* in front of it and *pas* after it, as in *Je n'ai pas le temps*
(I have no time). If the verb starts with a vowel or a silent *h*,
the *ne* will be shortened to *n'*.

Ne … plus rien (no more/nothing anymore) and *ne … pas du
tout* (nothing at all) are other variations of the negation.

Problems and Emergencies

Asking for Help

Aide-moi! ed mwah	Help me! *sing. inform.*
Aidez-moi! ed-ay-mwah	Help me! *sing. form./pl.*
Vous pouvez m'aider, s'il vous plaît? voo poo-vay med-day seel voo pleh	Can help me, please? *sing. form./pl.*
Tu peux m'aider? tew puh med-ay	Can you help me? *sing. inform.*
Pouvez-vous m'aider? poo-vay voo med-day	Can you help me? *sing. form./pl.*
Je peux vous aider? zhuh puh voo zed-ay	Can I help you? *sing. form./pl.*
Nous pouvons vous aider? noo poo-vohN voo zed-ay	Can we help you? *sing. form./pl.*
Je vous aide? zhuh voo zed	May I help you? *sing. form./pl.*
Vous avez besoin que je vous aide? voo zah-vay buh-zwaN kuh zhuh voo zed	Do you need my help? *sing. form./pl.*

Language Tip

The emergency number to dial in France is 15. Lines are open 24 hours a day and the operator will put you through to emergency services, *S.A.M.U.,* which coordinates all doctors and ambulances on duty. The number to dial for the fire department (*pompiers*) is 18.

Accidents

Something happened, but you were lucky:

Vous allez bien? voo zah-lay byaN   Are you all right?
sing. form./pl.

Ça va? sah vah   Everything OK?

Il vous est arrivé quelque chose? eel voo zet ah-ree-vay kul-kuh shohz   Did something happen to you? *sing. form./pl.*

Je vois qu'il ne vous est rien arrivé! zhuh vwah keel nuh voo zeh ryaN ah-ree-vay   From what I see, nothing happened to you! *sing. form./pl.*

Que s'est-il passé? kuh seh-teel pahs-say   What happened?

Ce n'est pas passé loin. suh neh pah pahs-say lwaN   That was close.

Il ne s'est rien passé. eel nuh seh ryaN pahs-say   Don't worry, nothing happened.

Vous avez besoin de quelque chose? voo zah-vay buh-zwaN duh kel-kuh shohz   Do you need anything? *sing. form./pl.*

Non merci, je n'ai besoin de rien. nohN mair-see zhuh nay buh-zwaN duh ryaN   No thanks, I don't need anything.

If, however, some damage was caused:

Pardon, mais je n'ai rien vu. pah-dohN meh juh nay ryaN vew   I am sorry, but I did not see anything.

Non, je n'ai pas vu. nohN zhuh nay pah vew   No, I did not see that.

Je ne pouvais pas voir.
zhuh nuh poo-vay pah vwah

I could not see anything.

Je ne pouvais pas vous voir.
zhuh nuh poo-vay pah voo vwah

I could not see you.
sing. form./pl.

Je ne pouvais rien voir du tout.
zhuh nuh poo-vay ryaN vwah dew too

I could not see anything
at all.

Ça m'est déjà arrivé.
sah meh day-zhah ah-ree-vay

That's happened to me
before.

Je n'y peux rien*.
zhuh nee puh ryaN

I couldn't help it.

Je n'y suis pour rien*.
juh nee swee poor ryaN

It's not my fault.

On va arriver pour vous aider. ohN
vah ah-ree-vay poor voo zed-ay

Help is on the way.
sing. form./pl.

Ce n'est pas beau à voir.
suh neh pah boh ah vwah

That doesn't look good.

Appelez la ... ! ah-play lah

Please call the ... !
sing. form./pl.

dépanneuse
day-pah-nuhz

police
poh-leess

---

* Idiomatic expressions:
  Je n'y peux rien. zhuh nee puh ryaN
  Je n'y suis pour rien.
  zhuh nee swee poor ryaN

I couldn't help it.
It's not my fault.

Language Tip

In rural France the *gendarmerie* fulfills the role of the police (*la police*). It is responsible for traffic accidents, mountain rescue operations, violations of the law, etc.

Loss and Theft

J'ai perdu quelque chose.
zhay pair-dew kel-kuh shohz

I have lost something.

J'ai perdu le …
zhay pair-dew luh

I have lost my …

sac
sahk

porte-monnaie
pawt-mun-ay

passeport
pahss-paw

collier
kawl-yay

C'est arrivé aujourd'hui.
set ah-ree-vay oh-zhoor-dwee

It happened today.

On est allé dans la chambre.
ohN et ah-lay dahN lah shahn-bruh

Somebody has been in my room.

Je n'ai plus rien! zhuh neh
plew ryaN

I have nothing left!

On nous a tout pris!
ohN noo zah too pree

They've taken everything from us!

J'ai tout perdu! zhay too pair-dew

I've lost everything!

Je vous dis que je n'ai rien vu!
zhuh voo dee kuh zhuh
neh ryaN vew

I'm telling you I did not
see anything!
sing. form./pl.

Visiting the Doctor

C'est à vous. set ah voo

You're next. *sing. form./pl.*

Qu'est-ce que je peux faire pour vous? kes kuh zhuh puh fair poor voo

What can I do for you?
sing. form./pl.

Que pouvons-nous faire pour vous? kuh poo-vohN noo fair poor voo

What can we do for
you? *sing. form./pl.*

Je ne vais pas bien.
zhuh ne veh pah byaN

I don't feel well at all.

Je ne vais pas très bien.
zhuh nuh veh pah treh byaN

I am not feeling too well.

Ça fait mal*. sah feh mahl

It hurts.

J'ai mal*. zhay mahl

I'm in pain.

J'ai très mal. zhay treh mahl

I'm in a lot of pain.

J'ai mal ici [pointing at it].
zhay mahl ee-see

It hurts here.

Où vous avez mal?
oo voo zah-vay mahl

Where does it hurt
you? *sing. form./pl.*

---

* Idiomatic expressions
   Ça fait mal sah feh mahl   it hurts
   J'ai mal. zhay mahl   I'm in pain

J'ai mal au ... seh mal o

My ... hurts.

bras
bra

pied
pje

ventre
vahN-truh

genou
zhuh-noo

Je peux voir où vous avez mal?
zhuh puh vwah oo voo zah-vay mahl

Can I see where it hurts you? *sing. form./pl.*

J'aimerais voir où ça vous fait mal. zhem-air-ray vwah oo sah voo feh mahl

I'd like to see where it hurts you. *sing. form./pl.*

Voyons ça! vwah-yohN sah

Let's take a look!

Je peux avoir quelque chose pour ça? zhuh puh ah-vwahr kel-kuh shohz poor sah

Can I have something for that?

Prenez ça et ça va aller mieux. pruh-nay sah eh sah vah ah-lay myuh

Take this and it will get better. *sing. form./pl.*

Quand vais-je aller mieux? kahN veh-zhuh ah-lay myuh

When will I be better?

Merci, ça fait du bien*. mair-see sah feh dew bee-aN

Thanks, that feels good.

---

* Idiomatic expression:
  Ça fait du bien. sah feh dew bee-aN   That feels good.

Country and Culture Tip

You'll recognize a French pharmacy (*pharmacie*) by the green sign. The regular opening hours are from 9 am to 7 or 8 pm. Every pharmacy will have a display with the nearest emergency pharmacy that is open at night.

Getting Lost

In case you have lost your way you can ask:

Pardon, mais je me suis perdu. ♂ pah-dohN meh zhuh muh swee pair-dew

Excuse me, I'm lost.

Pardon, mais je me suis perdue. ♀ pah-dohN meh zhuh muh swee pair-dew

Excuse me, I'm lost.

Je me suis perdu dans la ville. ♂ zhuh muh swee pair-dew dahN lah vee

I got lost in town.

Language Tip

When used in combination with a reflexive pronoun (e.g. *se, me*) *perdre* means, "to lose one's way". *Je me suis perdu* therefore means "I'm lost".

Vous êtes d'ici? voo zet dee-see

Are you from here?
sing. form./pl.

Vous pouvez me dire où est ..., s'il vous plaît? voo poo-vay muh deer oo eh ... seel voo pleh

Can you tell me where I can find ..., please?
sing. form./pl.

Pouvez-vous me dire où est … [destination]? poo-vay voo muh deer oo eh	Can you tell me where … is? *sing. form./pl.*
Où suis-je? oo swee-zhuh	Where am I?
Mais comment ai-je fait pour arriver ici? meh kohN-mohN ay-zhuh feh poor ah-ree-vay ee-see	How did I get here?
Je vais arriver trop tard. zhuh veh ah-ree-vay troh tahr	I will be late now.
Vous avez l'heure, s'il vous plaît? voo zah-vay luhr see voo pleh	Can you tell me what time it is, please? *sing. form./pl.*
Tu as l'heure, s'il te plaît? tew ah luhr seel tuh pleh	Can you tell me what time it is, please? *sing. inform.*
Quelle heure est-il? kel uhr eh teel	What time is it?

Other Problems

If something happens to you or your companion, you could say:

Il m'est arrivé quelque chose. eel meh tah-ree-vay kel-kuh shohz	Something happened to me.
Il s'est passé quelque chose. eel seh pahs-say kel-kuh shohz	Something happened.

Language Tip

When used in combination with a reflexive pronoun (e.g., *se*), the verb *passer* means "to happen".

J'ai cassé quelque chose.
zhay kahs-say kel-kuh shohz

I broke something.

Pardon, mais j'ai cassé le lit.
pah-dohN meh zhay kahs-say
luh lee

I am sorry, but I broke
the bed.

J'ai cassé votre ...
zhuh kahs-say voh-truh ...

I broke your ...
sing. form./pl.

télé
tay-lay

sèche-cheveux
sesh-shuh-vuh

appareil photo
ah-pah-ray foh-toh

If some appliance in your hotel room is broken say:

C'est cassé! seh kahs-say

It's broken!

Pardon, mais c'est cassé.
pah-dohN meh seh kahs-say

I am sorry, but this
is broken.

Le lit s'est cassé!
luh lee seh kahs-say

The bed came apart!

Pardon, mais le ... est cassé.
pah-dohN meh luh ... eh kahs-say

Excuse me, but the ...
is damaged.

radiateur
rah-dee-ah-tuhr

robinet
raw-bee-nay

fer à repasser
fair ah ruh-pahs-say

téléphone
tay-lay-fun

Dictionary

A

à ah at, to
A ce soir. ah suh swah Until tonight/this evening.
acheter ahsh-teh to buy
A demain! ah duh-maN Until tomorrow!
ai ay (I) have
ai besoin eh buh-zwaN (I) need
aide ed help
aider ed-ay to help
aidez ed-ay (you pl.) help
ai mal eh mahl (I) am in pain
aimer em-ay to like; to love
aimerais em-eh-ray (I) would like
aimeriez em-eh-ree-yay (you pl.) would like
aimerions em-air-ee-yohN (we) would like
allé ah-lay gone; driven
aller bien ah-lay bee-aN to go/fit well
allez ah-lay (you pl.) go
allons ah lohN (we) go
l'allumette ♀ lah-lew-met matchstick
l'Angleterre ♀ lahN-gluh-tair England
A plus tard! ah plew tahr See you later!
l'appareil photo ♂ lah-pah-ray foh-toh camera
appelé ah-play called
appeler ah-play to call
l'après-midi ♂ lah-preh-mee-dee afternoon

arrive ah-reev (he/she/it) arrives
arrivé ah-ree-veh arrived
arriver ah-ree-veh to arrive
arrivez ah-ree-veh (you pl.) arrive
as ah (you) have
A tout à l'heure! ah ttoo-tah luhr See you soon!
aujourd'hui oh-zhoor-dwee today
A une heure! ah ewn uhr Until one (o'clock)!
au plus oh plewss at most
au plus tard oh plew tahr (by) the latest
Au revoir. oh ruh-vwah Good-bye.
aussi oh-see also
avec ah-vek with
avez ah-veh (you pl.) have
avez besoin de ah-veh buh-zwaN duh (you pl.) need
avez mal ah-veh mahl (you pl.) hurt
avoir ah-vwah to have
avons besoin de ah-vohN buh-zwaN duh (we) need
passé pahs-say spent
avons ah-vohN (we) have
A vos souhaits! ah voh sway Bless you! (sneeze)

B

la baignoire lah ben-wahr bath tub
le bar luh bahr bar; pub
la barque lah bahrk boat
beau ♂ boh nice; pretty; handsome

beaucoup boh-koo much; many
belle ♀ bel nice; pretty
bien bee-aN good; well
boire bwahr to drink
bois bwah (I) drink
la boisson lah bwahs-sohN drink
bon ♂ bohN good; well
Bonjour. bohN-zhoor Good day./Good morning.
bonne ♀ bun good; well
Bonne journée! bun zhoor-nay Have a nice day!
Bonsoir. bohN swah Good evening/night.
les boules lay bool *French ball game*
le bras luh bra arm
bu bew drunk
le bus luh bewss bus
buvez bew-veh (you *pl.*) drink

C

ça sah that
le cabinet de toilette luh kah-bee-nay duh twah-let wash room
le cadeau luh kah-doh gift
ça fait sah feh that costs
Ça fait du bien. sah feh dew bee-aN That feels good.
ça fait mal sah feh mahl that hurts
le café luh kah-feh coffee; café
Ça me plaît. sah muh pleh I like that.
le camping luh kahN-ping camping

le Canada luh kah-nah-dah Canada
le canard luh kahN-nahr duck
Ça ne peut plus faire. sah nuh puh plew fair It can't go on like that.
la carafe d'eau lah kah-rahf doh a pitcher of water
la carte postale lah kahrt paws-tahl postcard
le casino luh kah-zee-noh casino
cassé kahs-say broken
casser kahs-say to break
Ça va? sah vah How's it going?
Ça va. sah vah Fine; OK
ce suh this; that; what
c'est seh that's
C'est à vous. set ah voo It's your turn.
cette set this
la cigarette lah see-gah-ret cigarette
la chambre lah shaN-bruh room
la chambre d'hôte lah shahN-bruh doht guest room
la chaussure lah shoh-sewr shoe
cher ♂ shair expensive
chère ♀ shair expensive
le chien luh shee-yaN dog
le chocolat luh sho-koh-lah chocolate
le cinéma luh see-nay-mah cinema; movie theater
le cintre luh saN-truh hanger
le cocktail luh cawk-tail cocktail

le **collier** luh kohl-yay
necklace
combien kohN-bee-aN
how many
Combien ça fait? kohN-
bee-aN sah feh How much
is it?
comment kohN-mohN how
Comment? kohN-mohN
Excuse me?
content kohN-tahN happy
la **crevette** lah kruh-vet
shrimp
le **croissant** luh kwah-sahN
croissant

D

dans dahN in; on
de duh from; of
déjà day-zhah already
le **déjeuner** luh
day-zhuh-nay lunch
demain duh-maN morning
demie duh-mee half
de mieux en mieux duh
myuh-zahN-myuh better
and better
la **dépanneuse** lah day-pah-
nuhz tow truck
De rien. duh ree-aN
Don't mention it.
des day *plural of* **un/une**
deux duh two
dimanche dee-mahnsh
Sunday
le **dîner** luh dee-nay dinner
dire deer to say
dis dee (I/you) say
la **discothèque** lah deess-
koh-tek discotheque

dit dee (he/she/it) says; said
dites deet (you *pl.*) say
d'où doo from where
la **douche** lah doosh shower

E

l'eau ♀ loh water
elle ell she
en ahN in; to
en tout ahN too all together
es eh (you *pl.*) are
l'escargot ♂ less-kah-goh
snail
est eh (he/she/it) is
est à l'heure et ah luhr is on
time
et eh and
les **États Unis** lay-zay-tah-
zew-nee United States
était ay-teh (he/she/it) was
êtes et (you *pl.*) are
être et-ruh to be
euro uhroh euro

F

faire fair to do; to make
faire à manger fair ah
mahN-zhay to cook
faire de la barque
fair duh lah bahrk to row
faire de la plongée fair duh
lah plohN-zhay to dive
faire de la randonnée fair
duh lah rahN-dun-ay to
walk; to hike
faire de la voile fair duh lah
vwahl to sail

faire de son mieux fair duh sohN myuh to do one's best

faire les magasins fair lay mah-gah-zaN to go window shopping

fais feh (I/you) do/make

faisons fuh-zohN (we) do/make

fait feh (he/she/it) does/makes

fait feh made

faites feht (you *pl.*) do/make

le fer à repasser luh fair ah ruh-pahs-say iron

la fleur lah fluhr flower

font fohN (they) make

les frites lay freet French fries

les fruits et légumes lay fwee eh lay-gewm fruit and vegetables

le fromage luh froh-mahzh cheese

G

la gendarmerie lah zhahN-dah-muh-ree (rural) police

le genou luh zhuh-noo knee

le gîte luh zheet (vacation) appartment

la glace lah glahss ice cream

grand grahN big; large

H

le hamburger luh ahm-bewr-gair hamburger

les haricots lay ah-ree-koh beans

l'heure ♀ luhr time; hour

l'hôtel ♂ loh-tel hotel

l'huître ♀ lwee-truh oyster

I

ici ee-see here

il eel he/it

Il fait beau. eel feh boh It is nice (the weather).

J

J'ai mal. zhay mahl I'm in pain.

je zhuh I

Je me suis perdu. zhuh muh swee pair-dew I'm lost.

Je n'en peux plus. zhuh nahN puh plew I can't go on.

Je n'y peux rien. zhuh nee puh ree-aN I couldn't help it.

Je n'y suis pour rien. zhuh nee swee poor ree-aN It's not my fault.

Je t'aime. zhuh tem I love you.

jeudi zhuh-dee Thursday

les journaux lay zhoor-noh newspapers

la journée lah zhoor-nay day

le jus de fruit luh zhew-duh-fwee fruit juice

L

la ♀ lah the

le ♂ luh the

les lay *pl.* the

la librairie lah lee-brair-ee
bookstore
le lit luh lee bed
les lits jumeaux lay lee
zhew-moh separate beds
loin lwaN far (away)
lundi laN-dee Monday

M

Madame mah-dahm
Mrs./Ms.; ma'am
Mademoiselle mahd-
mwah-zel Miss/Ms.
le magasin luh mah-gah-
zaN shop; store
mais meh but
mal mahl bad
mange mahNzh (I) eat;
(he/she/it) eats
manger mahN-zhay to eat
manges mahNzh (I/you) eat
mangez mahN-zhay (you
pl.) eat
m'appelle mah-pel my
name is
mardi mah-dee Tuesday
me muh me
la mer lah mair sea
merci mair-see thank you
Merci beaucoup! mair-see
boh-koo Thank you very
much!
mercredi mairk-ruh-dee
Wednesday
le métro luh may-troh
underground; subway
midi mee-dee midday; noon
mieux myuh better; nicer
minuit meen-wee midnight
moi mwah (to) me
moins mwaN before

Monsieur muh-syuhr Mr.; sir
la montagne lah mohN-
tahn-yuh mountain
le monument luh mohN-
new-mahN monument
la mousse au chocolat
lah mooss oh shoh-koh-lah
chocolate mousse
le musée luh mew-zay
museum

N

ne ... pas nuh ... pah not
ne ... pas du tout nuh ...
pah dew too not at all
ne ... plus nuh ... plew
no more
ne ... plus rien nuh ... plew
ree-aN nothing any more
ne ... que nuh ... kuh only
ne ... rien nuh ree-aN
nothing
non nohN no
nous noo we; us
nous nous appelons noo
noo-zah-plohN we are called
la nuit lah nwee night

O

l'office de tourisme ♂
loh-feess duh too-reez-muh
tourist office
on ohN one; we; you
On fait avec. ohN feh ah-vek
We'll make the most of it.
où oo where
oui wee yes
Oui, je vous en prie. wee
zhuh voo zahN pree Don't
mention it.

Oui, merci. wee mair-see
Yes, thank you.
ouvert oo-vair open
ouvre oo-vruh (he/she/it)
opens

P

le pain luh paN bread
le pantalon luh pahN-tah-
lohN pants; trousers
Pardon. pahr-dohN Excuse
me./I'm sorry.
la part de gâteau lah pahr
duh gah-toh piece of cake
passe pahss (he/she/it)
spends/passes (by)
passé pahs-say spent;
passed
le passeport luh pahss-paw
passport
passer pahs-say to spend;
to pass (by)
passer me voir pahs-say
muh vwah to visit me
passes pahss (I/you)
spend/stay
passez pahs-say (you *pl.*)
spend/pass by
passons pahss-ohN (we)
spend/pass by
la pellicule lah pel-ee-kewl
film (for the camera)
perdre pair-druh to lose
perdu pair-dew lost
petit puh-tee small
le petit-déjeuner luh puh-
tee day-zhuh-nay breakfast
le petit pois luh puh-tee
pwah pea
peut puh (he/she/it) can

peux puh (I/you) can
la pharmacie lah fahr-mah-
see pharmacy
le pied luh pee-ay foot
la pile lah peel battery
la piste de ski lah peest duh
ski ski slope
la plage lah plahzh beach
le plateau de fromage
luh plah-toh duh froh-mahzh
cheese platter
la plongée lah plohN-zhay
diving
plus plew more
le poisson luh pwahs-sohN
fish
la police lah poh-leess
police
la pomme de terre lah pum
duh tair potato
les pompiers le pohN-pee-
ay fire department
le porc luh paw pork (meat)
le porte-monnaie luh pawt-
mun-ay purse; wallet
le poulet luh poo-lay
chicken
pour poor for
pouvais poo-veh (I) could
pouvez poo-veh (you *pl.*)
can
pouvoir poo-vwah can; to
be able to
pouvons poo-vohN (we)
can
prendre prahN-druh to take
prendre du temps prahN-
druh dew tahN to take time
prendre le métro prahN-druh
luh may-troh to take the underground (subway)

prendre le temps prahN-druh luh tahN to take one's time

prendre un repas prahN-druh aN ruh-pah to eat a meal

prends prahN (I/you) take

prenez pruh-nay (you *pl.*) take

prenons pruh-nohN (we) take

le prêt-à-porter luh pret-ah-paw-teh ready-to-wear clothing

pris pree taken

le pull luh pewl sweater

Q

quand kahN when

le quart luh kahr quarter

que kuh that; how

Que c'est beau! kuh seh boh How nice!

quel kel which

quelle kel which

Quelle heure est-il? kel uhr eh-teel What time is it?

quelque chose kel-kuh-shohz something

Quel temps! kel tahN What (miserable) weather!

Qu'est-ce que c'est? kess-kuh seh What's that?

R

le radiateur luh rah-dee-ah-tuhr heater

la randonnée lah rahN-dun-ay hike; ride

le repas luh ruh-pah meal; dish

le restaurant luh res-toh-rahN restaurant

rien ree-aN nothing

la rivière lah ree-vee-yair river

le robinet luh roh-bee-nay water tap; faucet

S

le sac luh sahk (travel) bag

le sac à main luh sahk ah maN handbag

Salut. sah-lew Hello. Bye.

samedi sahm-dee Saturday

le S.A.M.U. luh ess-ah-em-ew French emergency services

Santé! sahN-teh Cheers!

le savon luh sah-vohN soap

se suh oneself

le sèche-cheveux luh sesh shuh-vuh hair dryer

le short luh shawr shorts

s'il te plaît seel tuh pleh please *inform.*

s'il vous plaît seel voo pleh please *form.*

le soir luh swah evening

sont sohN (they) are

sont en plus sohN tahN plewss (they) cost extra

le spectacle luh spek-tah-kluh show; spectacle

suis swee (I) am

T

la taille lah tah-yuh (cloth) size

t'appelles tah-pel (you) are called

tard tahr late

Tchin-tchin! tscheen-tscheen Cheers! (as toast)
te tuh you
la télé lah teh-lay tv
le téléphone luh teh-lay-fun telephone
le temps luh tahN weather; time
le théâtre luh teh-ah-truh theater
toi twah (to) you
la tomate lah toh-maht tomato
tout too all; everything
le train luh traN train
le tram luh trahm tram
très treh very
trop troh too
le t-shirt luh tee-shuhrt T-shirt
tu tew you
Tu en fais trop. tew ahN feh troh You exaggerate.

U

un ♂ aN one
une ♀ ewn one

V

va vah (he/she/it) goes
vais veh (I) go
vas vah (you) go
le vélo luh veh-loh bicycle
vendredi vahN-druh-dee Friday
le ventre luh vahN-truh belly; stomach
le verre luh vair glass

le verre d'eau luh vair doh glass of water
le vêtement luh vet-mahN clothing
la ville lah veel town; city
le vin luh vaN wine
le vin rouge luh vaN roozh red wine
Voilà! vwah-lah Here it is!
la voile lah vwahl sail
voir vwahr to see
vois vwah (I/you) see
voit vwah (he/she/it) sees
votre voh-truh you/yours
vous voo you
Vous en faites trop. voo zahN fet troh You exaggerate.
vous vous appelez voo voo-zah-play you are called
voyez vwah-yeh (you *pl.*) see
voyons vwah-yohN (we) see
vu vew seen

W

les WC lay doo-bluh-veh-say toilet; bathroom

Y

y ee there

0	1	2	3
zéro	**un/une**	**deux**	**trois**
zeh-roh	aN	duh	twah

4	5	6	7
quatre	**cinq**	**six**	**sept**
kah-truh	saNk	sees	set

8	9	10	11
huit	**neuf**	**dix**	**onze**
weet	nuhf	deess	ohNz

12	13	14	15
douze	**treize**	**quatorze**	**quinze**
dooz	trehz	kah-tawz	kaNz

16	17	18	19
seiz	**dix-sept**	**dix-huit**	**dix-neuf**
sehz	dee-set	deez-weet	deez-nuhf

20	21	22	30
vingt	**vingt et un**	**vingt-deux**	**trente**
vaN	vaN-tay-aN	vaN-duh	trahNt

31	40	41	50
trente et un	**quarante**	**quarante et un**	**cinquante**
trahNt-ay-aN	kah-rahNt	kah-rahNt-ay-aN	saNk-ahNt

51 **cinquante et un** saNk-ahNt-ay-aN	60 **soixante** swahss-ahNt	61 **soixante et un** swahss-ahNt-ay-aN
70 **soixante-dix** swahss-ahNt-deess	71 **soixante et onze** swahss-ahNt-ay-ohNz	80 **quatre-vingts** kah-truh-vaN
81 **quatre-vingt-un** kah-truh-vaN-aN	90 **quatre-vingt-dix** kah-truh-vaN-deess	91 **quatre-vingt-onze** kah-truh-vaN-ohNz
92 **quatre-vingt-douze** kah-truh-vaN-dooz	100 **cent** sahN	101 **cent et un** sahN-tay-aN
200 **deux cent** duh sahN	1000 **mille** meel	2000 **deux mille** duh meel

DAYS OF THE WEEK

| Monday **lundì** laN-dee | Tuesday **mardi** mah-dee | Wednesday **mercredi** mair-cruh-dee | Thursday **jeudi** juh-dee |
| Friday **venedri** vahN-druh-dee | Saturday **samedi** sahm-dee | Sunday **dimanche** dee-mahNsh | |